The King of Chicago

The King of Chicago

*The Incredible True Story of
a Jewish Orphan's Rise from
Despair to Triumph
in 1920s Chicago*

DANIEL FRIEDMAN

CARREL BOOKS

Copyright © 2017 by Daniel Friedman
First paperback edition, 2020

All rights reserved. No part of this book may be reproduced in any manner without the express written consent of the publisher, except in the case of brief excerpts in critical reviews or articles. All inquiries should be addressed to Carrel Books, 306 West 37th Street, 11th Floor, New York, NY, 10018.

Carrel Books books may be purchased in bulk at special discounts for sales promotion, corporate gifts, fund-raising, or educational purposes. Special editions can also be created to specifications. For details, contact the Special Sales Department, Carrel Books, 306 West 37th Street, 11th Floor, New York, NY, 10018 or carrelbooks@skyhorsepublishing.com.

Carrel Books® is a registered trademark of Skyhorse Publishing, Inc.®, a Delaware corporation.

Visit our website at www.skyhorsepublishing.com.

10 9 8 7 6 5 4 3 2 1

Library of Congress Cataloging-in-Publication Data is available on file.

Cover design by Rain Saukas

Print ISBN: 978-1-63144-082-3
Ebook ISBN: 978-1-63144-069-4

Printed in the United States of America

For my father Dan, my uncle Sol, and all the children of
the Marks Nathan Home

Contents

Preface	ix
Prologue	xv
One: Kasiel Skolnick	1
Two: Home Kids	21
Three: Rue des Beaux-Arts	54
Four: Home Kids—Two	62
Five: Arlington Park	81
Six: Apple Tree Lane	91
Seven: University Circle	125
Eight: Lake Shore Drive	135
Epilogue: Yad Vashem	149
Acknowledgments	151
Select Bibliography	153

Preface

The King of Chicago is the story I needed to write since the mid-1970s but gave up on many times because of my father's implacable refusal to tell me anything about his childhood, including his terrible upbringing in a Chicago Jewish orphanage called the Marks Nathan Home, a story I knew was full of violence and confusion. I wrote fifty or sixty pages when I was young, on my Smith Corona typewriter, single-spaced on onion skin, based on speculation and guesswork rather than history, but those passionate pages, a fiery love song to my magnificent father, vanished long ago, in one cardboard box or another, lost moving from apartment to apartment, from house to house, from city to city. It is an enormous unburdening for me, a great reckoning, to finally learn all the facts and tell the complete story of my father and his father, to have held onto the faint traces of them for all these years, and given them, at last, their final, proper burial.

My father, Dan Friedman, was a self-described "junk man," whose business, the Associated Salvage Company, was located on the South Side of Chicago within a few blocks of the Union Stock Yards, the vast meatpacking district that made Chicago, in Carl Sandburg's words, "Hog Butcher for the World." Anyone who had ever been near the Stock Yards during its heyday could not forget its awful stench, its reek of fresh blood and animal death. As bad as that smell, for a boy like me, was the unearthly noise coming from that corner of my father's city—the shrieking, bellowing sounds made by cattle as they were electrically prodded out of railroad boxcars into the slaughterhouses. Dad parked his Coupe de Ville in front of his plant, where we would see dozens of butchers smoking cigarettes as they walked home from work, their white jackets covered with blood. This was the unglamorous neighborhood where my tough father worked his entire lifetime and made his fortune.

The fact that he made a fortune of any kind was a bit of a miracle. My father was orphaned as a child and grew up in the Marks Nathan Home with his five siblings, not an ideal start in life, quite unlike the privileged start my father provided me. My father went from abject poverty to wealth in his lifetime, and he did this on his own, self-taught, with little formal education, no father, and no mentor save his older brother Sol, who got Dad out of the Home at age eleven and helped raise and shelter him. My father rose from the lowest rungs of society, mastered the city, and became its king. He protected me and elevated me far above him, achieving everything in life he set out to do, while showing and teaching me every secret inside the dark city of Chicago, every nuance, shade and shadow, high and low, and I loved him for it. He embodied Chicago for me. He was Chicago. And I loved them both. My father and his city.

His ascendancy did not happen overnight. His climb to the top took decades. His first thirty years of life were marred by false steps, fear, poverty, uncertainty, a move to Los Angeles after the war to start a film production company that went bad fast and decimated his meager savings, an ignominious return to Chicago, broke again, and lack of support from all but Sol, who showed him the way. In Sol, a great, loving older brother, he had his only teacher, but both of them had an uphill slog during the 1930s. It was the Depression, after all. I did not see the years of struggle with my own eyes. By the time I was born, Dad was already at the top of his game.

My mother, the beautiful Croatian girl he married, of pure Dalmatian stock—Adriatic people—was also born and raised "Back of the Yards," one of the toughest, grittiest neighborhoods in Chicago, and she was proud of it. Her brothers, my uncles, were boxers, neighborhood enforcers, GIs who served at Guadalcanal, the Battle of Henderson Field, and Iwo Jima, cogs in the Daley machine in peacetime, bluest of blue collars, plasterers and plumbers for a living. My mother's youngest brother, a war hero in the Pacific, taught me how to fight, to strike a foe squarely in the jaw or nose with a clenched fist and knock him out—like this, he showed me, low in a crouch, smiling at me, showing me how simple it was, a skill my Jewish father did not have and could not teach me.

Her parents spoke no English. My Croatian grandfather grew grapes in his backyard, made wine in his bathtub, and worked as a carpenter during construction of the Merchandise Mart. He was a heavy drinker and smoker and a silent type. I was the first person, on both sides of my family, to graduate university. My father's college went bankrupt during the Depression. For my mother, college was never an option. She went to work for the telephone company. Because she was so beautiful, she worked in public relations and posed for company photographs.

My mother did not know what she was thinking when she married a Jew. His Jewishness versus her Catholicism did not come up as an issue until many years later, when it became an issue for me. When I was a teenager seeking direction, a learned, flamboyant, and much respected rabbi I met at the University of Chicago told me I did not qualify as Jewish because my mother was Catholic, making me "an assimilate." I considered his words final, and me an outcast, until I arrived at my own solution many years later. Mom must have just blanked out on the whole Jewish question. The same for Dad. I don't blame them. Everyone was trying to be secular in America in 1945. Everyone in America just wanted to be American.

Dad was all over the place emotionally, high and low, giddy then tearful, and this mercurialness, which he understood and acknowledged, he blamed on his traumatic upbringing in the Home. Mom told me, unsympathetically I thought, that she'd met several men over the years who were contemporaries of Dad in the Home who were not as "nuts" as he, but that was Dad's view and he stuck by it. No one could tell him he wasn't damaged by the Marks Nathan Home. We did not know. We were not there. Her continued diminishment of the severity of his Home years, her disparagement of his principal story line, frequently caused the most vicious arguments between them, which badly unsettled me and which I hated to see. She was cruel to him. Despite his strength, Dad was fragile, and this I understood about him.

He cried every day. Doors were routinely slammed behind him. Then he would be in love with a piece of music, any opera by Puccini, and would play it at full volume, and he would weep at that, too. He introduced me to Franz Liszt's *Hungarian Rhapsodies,* which inspired me to dance around the room like a dervish in my pajamas. He was antisocial one moment, then the life of the party the next. He was sullen and withdrawn and needed bringing out, then he was holding court in the center of the room. I loved watching him, waiting for the switch to flip. He'd get lost in his reading or calculations and block out everything for hours. He would fight with my mother then bring home an enormous diamond or emerald bracelet for her that night, and all was forgiven, at least for the moment. He told me he wanted to divorce my mother when I was about ten, but when I begged him not to, pitifully, in tears, he relented and stayed married to her until his death.

Of course, the drugs did not help. As a little boy in the Home, he never slept, and as an adult, he developed a dependency on sleeping pills. Growing up in poverty without an intact family made him anxious and fearful, so he took anxiety meds. His physical health was never robust. He suffered from ulcers and took drugs for those, too. Dad once picked me up from a sleepover at a friend's house and fell asleep at the wheel. We were cruising north on the Edens Expressway at seventy-five miles per hour, and the heavy black Coupe de Ville started to drift toward the median. I was awake and alert and grabbed the wheel. He had dozed off. "It's those sleeping pills," he said. "Talk to me until we get home so I stay awake."

I preferred his light side to his dark side. I loved his jokes in Yiddish. Dad was American and born in Chicago, but like a Jewish Dr. Strangelove who couldn't help himself, he'd blurt out a flurry of Yiddish insults when he was excited or agitated. Our neighbor Goldstein was *farcocked* (an idiot). Mr. Weinberg across the street was *flablunget* (confused). *Zei gezunt* (be well) he would say to me with a kiss, when he was putting me to bed. Sometimes, entire sentences would emerge from the depths: *A mentsh zol leben shoin nor fun neigerikeit vegen* (a man should stay alive if only out of curiosity).

When his brain was on fire, he'd free-associate about money, markets, and the vanity of human wishes in a way I have never seen equaled. His brother Sol became one of Chicago's best courtroom litigators, but Dad's talk was second to none. These Friedman boys spoke with authority, gravitas, and from long experience in the school of hard knocks. No one knew reality better than they. They were grounded like no others. They had risen from the depths and lived to tell about it. This was my father at his best, when I was most proud of him. None of my friends' fathers could match his intellectual pyrotechnics, though none of them had started with less than he, and none of them loved their children more, even with his dramatic mood swings, which I had to master and understand because, after all, he was my father, as great a man as he could be, given his start in life in that black hole on the West Side of Chicago called the Marks Nathan Home.

Prologue

The greatest blizzard known to man paralyzed the indomitable city of Chicago on Thursday, January 26, 1967, when I was fifteen years old. The storm blew in overnight, taking everyone by surprise, including all the meteorologists of the day. Around five in the morning, in the complete darkness, my mother, frantic, woke me in my bedroom, my little brother sound asleep in his bedroom down the hall.

"Bernie Lynn just called," she told me, warm in my covers.

Bernie was a friend of Dad's, another junk man who raced cars over frozen lakes in northern Wisconsin during the winter months.

"He sounds like he is about to have a heart attack," Mom said. "He says there is so much snow he can't get his car out of the garage. He was trying to shovel but he can't make it. Go to the end of the street, Danny. Go now and get your father."

It was five o'clock in the morning and my father, typically, was in a big rush to get to work. Not working was unthinkable. Dad had walked through the snow to the corner so that Bernie would pick him up and, the theory was, they'd drive to work together on the far South Side, thirty miles away. That day, however, no one in Chicago was going anywhere.

I quickly got dressed and walked to the corner through wind and blinding snow unlike any I had ever seen. At first, I could not find Dad, and I panicked. Then, I saw him slumped down in a heap, already covered in a drift. I picked him up, shook off the snow, and carried him home. It was the least I could do, I loved him so.

Dad was babbling. I could feel his heart, against mine, racing.

"Don't do this to me, don't! Bernie's coming. I've got to get to work."

He was groggy and half asleep from all the pills and heavy narcotics he took every night before bed. He said he'd gotten tired walking through the snow and decided to just sit down and wait for Bernie. Then he had fallen asleep in the middle of the biggest snowstorm to ever hit Chicago. He could have died from hypothermia, right there in suburban Glencoe on Apple Tree Lane.

"Dad, Bernie is not coming. There will be no work today," I said.

I led Dad back to his bed and then crawled into my own, feeling good about myself. The score was far from even, but finally, I'd gotten to do one small thing for him after all the enormous love he had shown for me.

One

Kasiel Skolnick

Hyman Spector was a tall, slouching guy who always had a big cigar stuffed in the corner of his mouth. He and his pretty wife Mindy were our next-door neighbors for the great years on Apple Tree Lane, an entire street in an entire neighborhood of new split-level homes in Glencoe, Illinois, just north of Chicago. This neighborhood of ours was called Strawberry Hill, but there was no hill and no strawberries, only tall cottonwood trees shading a series of stagnant, algae-covered ponds known as the Skokie Lagoons. Seeds from the cottonwood trees blew over our neighborhood like so much cotton candy, into my mouth and hair as I pedaled my bike down the middle of Apple Tree Lane. I did not know the specific demographic at the time, but nearly every house in Strawberry Hill was occupied by the children and grandchildren of recent immigrants to America, all of them Eastern European Jews who had arrived on the Southwest Side of Chicago and then, gradually, as they took root, moved north along the shore of Lake Michigan.

Hyman and Dad were great friends. When they walked together on summer evenings, their riotous laughter could be heard around the block. I'd join them on my bicycle as they walked, tall Hy smoking a huge cigar and little Dad puffing away on his Parliament cigarettes. They laughed and smoked their way around the neighborhood almost every summer night, talking to each other so fast I had trouble keeping up with what they were saying.

One Saturday morning Hy called the house and asked Dad to come over immediately to see something important, a new business project he was working on. My father sprang from the sofa and brought me along to help him consider this deal. So we walked next door, Dad and I—typical of Dad to involve me in everything, to get me thinking about business from an early age. It was midsummer, 1963, and I was twelve years old.

Mr. Spector had just purchased the rights to manufacture in the United States a novelty called the Lava Lite, and had a working prototype of this amazing device in the blacked-out basement of his house on Apple Tree Lane. This Lava Lite, like the tens of millions that came later, was a tall, cone-shaped glass vessel that contained different types of wax, which, when heated from below by a special bulb, floated around in odd shapes and colors like a precursor of what I would later know as an LSD trip.

I had never seen the fun-loving Mr. Spector so intense. He had an insane, ecstatic look on his face, a mad scientist in his dark basement, furiously smoking as he watched the weirdly glowing Lava Lite do its thing.

"What do you think, Dan?" Hy asked my dad. "We need just ten grand more. Then we are going into immediate production for the entire country. Can I count you in?"

Dad wasn't as certain about this curiosity called the Lava Lite. He looked at it quizzically and was pleasant and polite but nonetheless noncommittal. He did not say out loud that he thought his friend Hyman Spector was a complete idiot for backing such an inanity as this, but I could read his mind and knew what he was thinking.

We left Hyman's house without a deal and quickly walked home. Dad asked me what I thought.

"I really don't know what to think, Dad," I said.

"It's completely crazy," Dad said emphatically. "Nobody needs a Lava Lite."

The emphasis was on "need." In Dad's world, people only bought stuff they needed. Dad was speaking from his own experience growing up on the Southwest Side of Chicago when people barely had enough money for food and clothing. Even at age twelve I knew that about him.

So just like that we whiffed on one of the greatest crazes of 1960s America, a get-rich-quick scheme like no other. It turned out people did buy stuff they didn't need, lots of it.

Every morning, Dad drove the big Coupe de Ville on the Edens Expressway from our house in Glencoe to his plant on the far South Side of Chicago. Only a few months after that meeting, a huge Lava Lite factory was built on Irving Park Road near the expressway, with a fully operating forty-foot-tall Lava Lite perched on the roof, taunting us every time we drove into the great city. Our relationship with Hy

Spector remained friendly, but it changed. We saw much less of him as his business exploded. He wasn't seen smoking cigars, walking leisurely around Apple Tree Lane any longer. He was busy on Irving Park Road cranking out Lava Lites. I bought one myself, put it in my bedroom, and loved the thing, like every other kid.

For me, these were the best of times. I had everything I desired. We may have passed on the Lava Lite venture, but life on Apple Tree Lane was nearly perfect that summer of 1963.

Such happiness was not always the case for the men in our family. In terms of happiness, 1963 was a great anomaly. In fact, it might have been the greatest year in the previous hundred.

Sixty years earlier, on February 12, 1903, a person of great importance to me, but of no notoriety or consequence then, and during his short lifetime, arrived alone in the Port of Baltimore aboard the SS *Breslau*, in steerage class, after a sixteen-day ocean crossing from Bremen, Germany. The 1,660 steerage passengers traveled in miserable conditions below deck, twenty people to a compartment, twelve toilets between them. Sixty more passengers traveled in relative comfort above deck in cabin class.

This passenger arriving solo, emerging on these shores alone, was my heroic, trailblazing grandfather. He had a magical name, Kasiel Skolnick, and he was the founder of our family. Our American history began with him, his decision to escape

Poland, his solitary journey across northern Europe to the port of Bremen, his ocean voyage in midwinter, and his arrival in Baltimore on his twenty-second birthday.

The name was Skolnick. Kasiel Skolnick.

He was just five feet one and a half inches tall.

Kasiel's emergency passage to America and my father's childhood in the Marks Nathan Home was our Holocaust story, peripheral, a sidebar perhaps, but ours nonetheless. Dislocated, desperate, dismembered people, families and nations in rags—this was our starting point in America, but better than everything we left behind.

According to the ship manifest, my grandfather was completely impoverished. His personal property—his worldly goods catalogued at the port of arrival—amounted to three dollars, a suitcase, and the clothes on his back. Kasiel Skolnick was a Hebrew, a tailor by profession, and unmarried. He could read and write basic English, and his health was noted as "good." The money he had on him was running out fast. His ocean journey to America could have cost twenty dollars. With the remaining cash, he had to figure out how to get from Baltimore to Chicago to join his sister, Sarah. As his grandson, intimately familiar with his DNA, I'm certain he improvised his way across the country.

―――

"Danny!" my father would always tell me with the greatest urgency when I was a small boy. "Forgive me! I make a lot of mistakes. Please don't hold it against me! I don't know how to be a good father because I never had one myself! Please forgive me. I am a poor, uneducated schmuck who grew up in the Marks Nathan Home. I know nothing about fatherhood. Please don't hold it against me!"

This was my father's standard response whenever I asked about his childhood, his Home years, or his father, the man we later knew as Kasiel Skolnick. My father mounted a massive defense—it flew up like an enormous shield to deflect my most innocent and childlike inquiry. I wanted to know how we got here, as any kid would.

But it was impossible to hold anything against my passionate, energetic father. I loved him with all my heart.

"Dad," I would tell him, mustering all my energy, as small as I was, a young boy looking into his father's agitated, often tearful, face. "You are the world's best father. I would not trade you for any."

He was my father. I was his son. There was nothing else.

And I meant it. I put my arms around him and hugged him and took in his scent—musty and bitter, a scent that repelled me, a scent that I loved. It was a lurid scent of a lurid man, born and raised in Chicago. When I crawled into his bed in the early mornings after he left for work, I was appalled and shocked by the sharp and bitter scent of his pillows and bedding, not understanding where it came from or how it was produced, but then I enveloped myself in it, knowing it was him, wrapping myself in my father's strength. From the earliest age I turned the tables on my father, I loved him so. By twelve I had become his father. I could do this for him because I had a father who showed me how to love. Having been loved by him, however clumsily, I knew how to love in return, and I knew it was my job to protect and care for the man who had so protected and cared for me, especially from my mother, his wife, who was cruel and undermined his central life story. That was our pact, and it lasted until the day he died. It lasts until now, in fact, because it's my love for him that drove me to uncover the truth and tell the story of his childhood, which he barely survived in the giant, powerful, and unforgiving city of Chicago.

Dad had a father, just not the superstar dad he wanted. Dad never knew his father and certainly did not appreciate him. Tiny, brave, swarthy, unknown, decisive, dirt-poor Kasiel Skolnick, who left Dad nothing but bitterness, was his father. Kasiel died in 1916, one year after my father's birth. His death sent my father's life, and the lives of Dad's five brothers and sisters, into a tailspin that nearly killed them all. As for me, I knew virtually nothing of this incandescent grandfather of mine until I was nearly sixty years old. I tried my entire lifetime to learn his story but encountered roadblocks, obfuscation, lies, and denial, and had given up hope of ever discovering any information, any facts, about Kasiel Skolnick. I wasn't even certain of his real name until 2014. This hole in me—not knowing my grandfather, my father's unwillingness to share with me what little he knew—was something I adjusted to and learned to live with. Finally, it took four equally determined cousins working together nearly two years to unearth the truth about him, and even now his biography is incomplete. Parts of the story we will just never know, such as his cause of death, and that's all right, we are finally at peace with that.

Little Kasiel, the grandfather who forged my future in America, arrived in the United States in 1903 to launch his attack upon the New World. What was he thinking? How desperate must he have been? Many of the Poles, Lithuanians, and Jews on board the *Breslau* with him arrived with less, some with as little as fifteen cents. Their occupations were invariably listed as "laborer" or "none," and they were heading to join relatives in the Midwest: Chicago, Detroit, Cleveland, Steubenville. They were going where the jobs were, into the teeming, bleeding heart of heavy American manufacturing and industry, where many would be chewed up and spit out, living a life no better, no easier, than the one they left behind in Eastern Europe. The Jews on board the *Breslau* might have eluded the vicious pogroms and the Holocaust in Europe, but they could not avoid two World Wars and the Great Depression in America. For two generations, my family barely made it. Families, like nations, have trajectories. For us, February 1903 was low ebb. In the years to come, equally desperate chapters would follow.

Kasiel's destination, according to the *Breslau* manifest, was 606 West 43rd Street in Chicago, the home of his brother-in-law, Isaac Serolnik Isaacson, already married to Kasiel's sister, Sarah. This couple, Mr. and Mrs. Isaacson, would later appear as a bleak footnote in the childhood lives of their future, yet unborn, nieces and nephews.

This was a very big year for my grandfather, the biggest. Within months of his arrival in Chicago he married my grandmother, Jenny Pinckovitch, also newly arrived from Poland, a boarder with the Isaacsons on West 43rd Street. She was a tall, patrician-looking Ashkenaz whose pure white skin and intelligent features contrasted so sharply with Kasiel's dark, classically Sephardic features, his full lips; olive skin; hooded eyelids; heavy black eyebrows; and tight, short-cropped black hair. At 5'6", the elegant, lily-white Jenny towered over her proud and robust husband. Kasiel married far above his station in life. Jenny Pinckovitch, his new bride, had a large, well-connected, and industrious family already firmly established and going places in Chicago.

Then, within weeks or months of marrying Jenny, Kasiel Skolnick legally changed his name to Samuel Friedman. He and Jenny became Mr. and Mrs. Sam Friedman. Like that, Kasiel Skolnick vanished nearly forever.

Kasiel Skolnick is now a spell and incantation for me. The name resonates as something familiar but long forgotten, a name we were once known by. It's not alien or strange to me; it's true. But my grandfather had a plan for himself in America and *Kasiel* was not part of the plan. *Kasiel* would not cut it in Chicago, not then, not in 1903. A five-foot-one-inch Hebrew tailor named Kasiel Skolnick wouldn't make it halfway down the street among the German and Irish immigrants who populated the city. There was no future on the Southwest Side of Chicago for Kasiel Skolnick. How he got to Samuel and Friedman we will never know, but his new name was an inspired choice for the time and place. His was a brilliant and farsighted rebranding effort, and all subsequent generations thanked him for it. I'm grateful not to have gone through life named Skolnick, even though the name is mine.

Kasiel was the ultimate realist. Acute awareness of his surroundings was his defining characteristic. He knew Europe was bad news for the Jews, so he risked his life and left the continent. Chicago required subtler corrections. His name change served his family well but made genealogical work enormously complicated generations later.

———

Since his death in 1916, unbeknownst to us, Samuel lay in an unmarked grave, under a small, plain slab, in the vast Waldheim Cemetery on the far West Side, buried among 150,000 other Chicago Jews. Waldheim is a world unto itself. It covers over two hundred acres of mausoleums and crumbling, haphazardly arranged headstones on both sides of busy Des Plaines Avenue. In 2013, after painstaking research, my cousin Gregory, a Chicago lawyer like his father, my uncle Sol, somehow located Samuel's grave and had a proper headstone installed:

<blockquote>
In Memory of
Our Grandfather
Samuel Friedman
February 12, 1881–May 2, 1916
</blockquote>

A couple of months after moving back to the city, after an absence of thirty-eight years, on one of those damp gray Chicago mornings with plastic bags the only foliage in the leafless trees of early spring, the wind blowing, the naked trees shaking hard, unseen air traffic coming in low and loud toward O'Hare, I stood in a puddle over my grandfather's new headstone in Waldheim saying Kaddish with Gregory, just the two of us alone there. After we completed the prayer, we embraced one another, standing atop our grandfather's plot in the rain, no one else in the vast cemetery that dreary morning. Gregory's scent, holding him closely, was of my father. Gregory is my blood relative. It was no surprise. Gregory brought my father, his father, and our grandfather back to life.

I moved back to Chicago to reclaim these men and to follow their scent. It's more common to move where you have grandchildren than back to the place where your grandparents are buried, but that's what I did. Counterintuitive, I admit. To Chicago, of all places, that brutal, magnificent city, so big and bad, populated for me by a legion of ghosts, my family in the majesty of their immigrant rags and hope, astonished at their good fortune to escape the old world, afforded the brilliance of a new morning in a kitchen on South Halsted Street, in a house that has long since been leveled. I needed a new start, too.

Divorce in a small town is painful in any number of ways, your wounds exposed to an entire population free to conjecture at your expense. At such moments, small towns are at their worst. Everyone on Main Street has taken a position, like it is a political contest; few express outright support, but many revel in your distress, unable to disguise their schadenfreude, like the realtor eager to list your house now that the marriage is finally kaput after years of effort. Soon, the calls begin. Intimate friends of your ex-wife, or so you thought, women you have known for decades, women once married to your friends, or women you knew as mothers of your children's friends, now ring at cocktail hour, Chianti in hand, purring with invitations. When this becomes your romantic default mode, it's time to move on.

And so I told myself, when this just happened to me: it isn't too late; you're not too old. So I returned to Chicago where I had a right to be, where my people were buried and I could reside in anonymity among the Miesian high-rises and the few survivors of my nearly forgotten childhood—including Gregory, Sol's son, whom I hadn't seen in years but who had become vitally important to me, as well as my other Friedman cousins and a few very ancient friends from Glencoe, Illinois, who took me up again as if I had never left, though I had been away more than forty years.

For Gregory and me, this story began when we started asking ourselves questions of great significance to men over the age of sixty, such as: Why did our grandfather lie in an unmarked grave? Was there any truth to the "Skolnick" rumors we heard whispered over the years? Why did our fathers never speak of him? Was there something shameful about his life or death that made him unspeakable, as we sensed or feared? Did my father tell me he died of syphilis, or did I only dream this? The fear that my grandfather died of a venereal disease too shameful for discussion shadowed my lifetime. Standing there, praying together at his graveside, we still did not know much about our grandfather.

Did he lie in an unmarked grave because he was a criminal? Was his life so ordinary as to be unworthy of note? Was it possible to determine the facts of his life one hundred years after his death and in the absence of evidence beside a few documents, one photograph, and a ring? Would our grandfather's short and turbulent life simply vanish, as my father's huge life was now fast disappearing, too, my father's and my uncles' massive footprint on the city of Chicago all but faded in the soot? No, not if we had anything to do with it.

Kasiel was our first American person and Chicago was our first American place, wherever we happened to live afterward. Kasiel's is the story of our Chicago start-up, and the story of his children is Chicago's story before and after World War II. He authored my Chicago baby boomer story, and he helped launch my son, founder of software companies in Boston and San Francisco, who never lived in Chicago, but who is the great-grandson of Kasiel Skolnick.

The grandfather I never knew or heard discussed by anyone, at any time, may have accomplished more in 1903 than I have in my lifetime. He changed the course of history. And without the equal courage and resilience of my father, Kasiel's youngest son, I would never have made it either.

Kasiel and Jenny, my dark little grandfather and his patrician bride, had great chemistry, easily discernable from ample physical evidence. They produced seven children in seven years, my dad the last and the runt of the litter. One of their children died at birth.

"Don't try to tell me you're not horny," Augie March's brother tells him in Saul Bellow's novel.

"We all are, in our family."

When I see the only existing photograph of Kasiel, I see an almost embarrassingly horny little guy with that magisterial Ashkenazi grandmother of mine who allowed herself to be taken and knocked up by her vigorous husband every year. He was irresistible, a force of nature, and so was my swashbuckling father. As far as I know—and I have made many inquiries with the utmost discretion—it's one of our most pronounced genetic traits, which endures today in many lucky branches of our family tree.

In that lone surviving photograph, Kasiel wears a gold signet ring, the ring that Gregory now wears and treasures, passed somehow from Kasiel to Sol, Kasiel's oldest son, and from Sol to Gregory. This ring is the only item we have that once belonged to Kasiel. Gregory wears it with full appreciation of the vast distance the ring has traveled.

This photograph is a studio portrait of Kasiel's immigrant family knocking loudly on the front door of America, a family full of promise circa 1911. Kasiel (by then Sam) and Jenny are dressed in their finery, Sam in an immaculate jacket and tie and pocket watch, Jenny in a long black dress, wearing earrings, with several gold necklaces, and her hair attractively pulled back from her face. Three of their children, Annette, Sol, and Minna, in white gowns and overshirts, pose alongside their parents, with three more still to come. These first three children bear no resemblance to Sam. That would change when my father was born five years later. My father was the spitting image of Kasiel Skolnick.

Kasiel fled the shtetl of Knyszyn, midway between Bialystok and Grodno in Northeast Poland. This region, the Pale of Settlement, a vast Eastern European Jewish prisoner system and outdoor ghetto, was always terrible news for Jews. Today, the Jews don't go back. There are no reunions held there. We go to Maui or Turks and Caicos instead.

For people like Kasiel, this was the world's worst neighborhood at the start of the twentieth century, which only got worse for those who chose, for whatever reason, to remain. By 1942, with few exceptions, all of Knyszyn's remaining Jews would be dead, executed by the Nazis with the eager collaboration of the village's non-Jewish population. After the Jews of Knyszyn were at last eradicated, the townspeople demolished the synagogue and former homes of the Jews, using the building stones to repair or construct additions onto their own village houses. Today, there is no evidence that thousands of Jews lived there for hundreds of years, save for a few barely legible headstones in the Jewish cemetery. At Treblinka, the nearby death camp, there is a stark memorial of seventeen thousand stones that symbolize the villages and towns of Jews that were gassed there. One of the stones at Treblinka is inscribed "Knyszyn."

My grandfather got out of Knyszyn in the nick of time. The pogrom of 1906 took place three years after his departure for Chicago and was described by the *New York Times* as "a general massacre of the Jews, slaughtered like sheep." Seven hundred were murdered that day. Two months later, in Bialystok, 2,600 Jews were murdered. In 1941, when the Nazis seized Poland, the complete liquidation of the Jews began. The SS Einsatzgruppen shot Jews en masse, 5,200 in Bialystok alone. In little Knyszyn, on Januray 11, 1942, three hundred of the Gestapo cordoned off the village, set fire to the synagogue full of worshippers, and herded the town's remaining Jews into the Chervony Jar, the "Red Ravine," a slimy pit of death, where they were all executed by shooting. Jews that somehow escaped the Gestapo that day were quickly deported to Auschwitz and Treblinka. Hundreds of thousands of Jews lived in Bialystok, Knyszyn, and Grodno around 1900. Today there are none. More than three million Polish and Russian Jews were murdered by the Nazis between September 1939 and January 1945, on top of all the murdering of Jews by their non-Jewish neighbors during the preceding centuries.

Knyszyn, this wretched place, population 2,800 today, always hell on earth for Jews, launched an image campaign in 2015 to rewrite its history as a culinary destination. City fathers, incredibly, are crediting the shtetl with the invention of the knish, a Hebrew meat and vegetable pie and great nostalgia food item. The town invented the knish, they claim, and it now hosts an annual summer knish festival, even though the citizens of Knyszyn helped the Gestapo murder all the people who supposedly created the knish in the first place. This knish festival is an outrageous way to attract tourists without memory and remake the town's bloody history. I asked one of the festival judges via email if the festival included tours of the Chervony Jar and site of the destroyed synagogue but received no reply.

The knish festival in Knyszyn is a Mel Brooks routine: grandchild of Jew who fled town in terror returns to Knyszyn on heritage tour, wins knish-eating contest, sings late into the night over campfire, arm in arm with the locals, yucking it up with the grandchildren of mass murderers.

But that is where we came from and that is what Kasiel Skolnick fled. He chose well. No Jew survived Knyszyn. In Chicago, he was free.

That I spent my entire childhood in idyllic Glencoe, Illinois, during the Eisenhower administration was not so much a miracle as it was the result of my grandfather's ability to think on his feet and get the hell out of town. Kasiel sensed trouble on the horizon and acted fast. He got on the *Breslau* and left Europe behind. My father made it his business to predict the future. On the backs of these two alert men my life was built. My children and grandchildren and subsequent generations need to know what we owe them, which is nothing short of everything.

Dad spared me his childhood memories of Chicago, which I was desperate to know.

"Father," I'd say, looking into his hazel eyes and probing, "what was your childhood like? Did you like the White Sox or the Cubs? Did you have a bicycle? Did you have a house like we do? Did you go to the movies? What did you read?"

Yes, he read, no, he never had a bicycle, and yes, he played chess. Sol was a ranked chess player who played competitively, fifty boards at a time, winning them all. I liked these few details but they were all I got.

Wildly swinging both fists, punching the air, my little dad waved off questions about his past, too painful to answer. He cried openly around me when he looked me in the eye; when I pushed him about his childhood or his father that he and I had never known, he'd bawl, age fifty. My tough, smart dad, born and raised on the Southwest Side of Chicago, who'd seen it all, would openly weep before me, his twelve-year-old son. And then I would cry too. I knew he was hurt badly, so after many years of loving, natural, boyish curiosity about my father and his father, I finally stopped asking him anything.

But still I wondered. How horrible could it have been? We were alive and living in leafy Glencoe. Soon I'd be attending New Trier High School, the elite of elites. Life was not so bad. In the process of not asking, I gradually gave up my right to know our history, and this lack of knowledge haunted me, because I was certain there was something of profound shame. *Please just tell me all of it, if only once, please just spit it out. I can take it.* But he wouldn't or couldn't tell me.

My father would not speak of his father, but his feelings about his mother were plain. He loathed Jenny. I never knew a man in fact or fiction who hated his mother as much as my father hated his. He was dutiful and paid her way, but he detested her. Every Saturday morning he'd drive me to her apartment for an obligatory family visit, and every Saturday, a mere five minutes into it, just as I was settling down on the floor with a game or a book, he'd pull me up by the arm, furious at something she said.

"We're leaving!" he'd shout, slamming the apartment door on the way out.

"Dad," I'd ask him in the car, "what happened? What's wrong? Why are you so mad at Grandma Jenny?"

"Danny Boy, what kind of mother would put her children in an orphanage, I ask you?" Dad shouted at me from behind the wheel. "What kind of unnatural mother is that?"

This was the headline I heard repeatedly, and I agreed with him. Only a monster could have done that to her children. I could not fathom his pain. No matter how terrible the circumstances, no mother should abandon her offspring. With no father, my father wanted and needed his mother, but she moved him and his siblings into a huge orphan home on the West Side of Chicago, where they lived for years.

Sam died in 1916 at age thirty-six, but Jenny lived on Lake Shore Drive with a view of Belmont Harbor until ninety-five in an apartment paid for by her sons. Jenny spoke Yiddish and German only, no more than a few words in English, even after seventy-five years in America. Ever the family historian, I needed to question her, too, and she was even less forthcoming than her youngest son. On one such visit, my father, in his reluctant but fluent Yiddish, a language he wished he could forget because he had mastered it during his years in the Marks Nathan Home, translated a few of my questions.

"Ma," he shouted across the room at her. "Danny wants to know what your childhood was like in Poland." As if—my son is a complete imbecile for asking such a cockamamie question.

"Ah." Jenny's eyes got big.

She understood the naïve nature of the request coming from the small boy seated on the floor of her apartment. She knew, in some far-off grandmotherly way, that I needed to hear a story, a family myth. Her impenetrable, guttural Yiddish was absolutely foreign to me. She could have been speaking Mandarin.

"Like cowboys," Dad translated for me with a smirk. "They were like cowboys." Dad rolled his eyes at the inanity of her reply.

Even at thirteen, I knew this response was a total fabrication. There were no cowboys in Poland. Jenny knew I was an American kid and gave an answer she thought I'd understand.

Clearly Jenny did not want to discuss her personal history either. This attempted interaction is the only one I remember with my grandmother. She looked over my head as if I wasn't in the room. She had no interest in me. But she was interested in my father to the extent that she always had a litany of issues to take up with him on these Saturday morning visits, which I could not understand and which always infuriated him.

When we were in the black Coupe de Ville driving home, I told Dad that Jenny's response to my question was completely inadequate, which only made him more furious. He turned and faced me from the driver's seat.

"Danny Boy! We were poor schmucks! Don't you get that?"

It was sinking in, but I wasn't sure what that meant.

"I'm a poor schmuck from the Marks Nathan Home," Dad used to say when I asked about his father or his mother or his years in the orphanage.

"Don't hold it against me."

By this time, however, Dad was already well on the way to becoming a wealthy man, even without the Lava Lite deal. He was no longer a poor schmuck—far from it.

"I'm a poor schnook from the Home. Please leave it at that."

This was the technique Dad used to end serious conversations with me, his coup de grace, his forceful gambit when faced with a compelling counterpoint that required extra thought on his part. Dad punched through argument, punched through life. He was not going to learn from me but I was learning from him. I have him and the Marks Nathan Home to thank for my compassion for the distraught, my ability to listen to the ones I love, and to calmly endure the most insane argument. He taught me everything I know.

Two

Home Kids

My grandfather came to America penniless and died young after fathering seven children in seven years, one who died at birth. My father, his youngest, spent his entire childhood in an orphanage on the West Side of Chicago. This was my history of America, the world I was born into, me, a tiny kid with a view out the back seat window of my father's Coupe de Ville as he plied the Edens Expressway, always in the fast lane, always exceeding the speed limit, his natural tempo, never ticketed, fat Cadillac tires rhythmically pounding the pavement, as we made our way, father and son, into the giant city of Chicago.

Everything about Chicago scared the hell out of me as a boy and enchanted me as a man. My greatest fear growing up was that Chicago would require me to become a bad guy, a criminal in fact, to at least keep my head above water, to maintain pace with the authentic bad guys who ruled the city and were its chiefs. I did not want that to be my future. I wanted to be one of the good guys. But it was nearly impossible to avoid rackets and minor criminal activity even as a boy in Chicago. You had to screw somebody over, or you just weren't alive. You had to shoplift, a competitive sport among thirteen-year-olds, even in privileged Glencoe. We shoplifted from every store. Every transaction in Chicago had a winner and a loser, starting with trading baseball cards. My father showed me I had better be tough, I had better be quick, very quick, to be prepared for the chaos to come, that I had better know what the fuck was going on because something terrible and unimaginable was on the immediate horizon. Sure enough, six or seven months after moving back to Chicago, I started having recurrent dreams about revolvers. In Chicago, I dreamt, I'd pull the trigger without hesitation or remorse.

The details of my father's life thrilled and horrified me as a child, as sketchy and incomplete as those details were. His was a gaudy Chicago romance, bigger and badder by far than *Guys and Dolls*. His father was a "bum," who amounted to "nothing." His mother a heartless woman who condemned five of her six surviving children to life inside the cavernous Marks Nathan Home, the red brick monstrosity occupying an entire city block at 1550 South Albany Avenue, still there today, now a home for the insane, where she put them all when Sam died, once each child met the minimum enrollment age of five. My father turned five January 5, 1920. The next month Jenny completed an intake form and application without missing a beat, and Dad was moved into Marks Nathan, the youngest and smallest kid in the entire institution. What was his first night like? How was it explained to him where he was being taken, and who did the explaining? What great fear must he have felt? What terror? "Wee Danny Friedman" he was called in *The Echo*, the Home's newspaper.

Dad didn't have a lot going for him. On top of all this, he was a chronic bed-wetter, shamed for it every morning he woke up in Marks Nathan. That he survived the Home is a miracle. That I managed to see the light of day is a miracle, too.

I didn't want to be a Jew, but I am. I did not want this to be my story, but it's the only one I've got. In America there was the dream that everyone would be the same, but of course that's not true. All boys wanted to be Chuck Connors or Steve McQueen or play third base for the Cubs. I wanted to be like Ralph Lauren, stylish and without religion. I tried to continue my father's fiction, his lesson to me, that we are all Americans here, not Jews. Kasiel Skolnick believed it too. He changed his name to Sam. But this fiction of Dad's was wrong. Almost everywhere I went in the small towns of America, people who were not Jews reminded me within minutes of meeting them that I am one. That's a difference between my father and me. Dad was only comfortable with the Jews despite what he decried as their terrible table manners. I was better educated and more widely traveled than my father and lived among the *goyim*, penetrating their reaches and private enclaves, thinking I was one of them because I joined their clubs and slept with their women. I did not have to sort out that Jewish shit. My dad married a *shiksa*. My beautiful mother was Catholic. I was assimilated. Certain rabbis considered me completely non-Jewish for this reason. I was American. End of story. But the story would never end.

In Virginia, married into a First Family of Virginia, bringing fresh mojo and high sperm count to several extinct bloodlines, I was the Big Jew, front and center, naked in my Jewishness but with no bar mitzvah money and only a handful of Yiddish words in my vocabulary. The pointed questions and comments, in the most refined of Virginia settings, in paneled clubrooms or hilltop eighteenth-century estates, always took me off guard. At first I thought these otherwise well-dressed, well-educated people were simply joking. I'd pause and smile at them, and wait for them to laugh. But they didn't laugh. There was no laughter. They were always dead serious.

"Why are Jews so tribal?" This from the publisher of a chain of fifty daily newspapers and the owner of seven television stations.

"At St. Paul's, I had a piano teacher from New York named Mr. Friedman," a blonde beauty told me at a cocktail party.

By the time we made it to the fourth or fifth hole on the golf course at the country club, someone would ask me, "What do you think Netanyahu's next move is going to be with Hezbollah?"

Over the years, I had come to expect these questions so I was not unprepared for them.

"Not sure, but I'll ask next time I see him."

"I'm a big supporter of Israel, I want you to know that."

I was drawing back my putter.

"Nice to know, thanks."

"Yeah, Israel is our first line of defense in the Middle East."

"Glad we're making it safe for you in Hilton Head."

The anti-Semitism thrust upon me in the little town took many forms, almost all benign. Many were simple cases of bird-watching.

"Oh, you must be a Jew. Have not seen one since rooming with one at Duke. Let me tell you about him."

The few beleaguered local Jews in Charlottesville did nothing to help the cause. Most of them suffered from terrible cases of concealed, heavily camouflaged identity.

"Are you Jewish?" I asked someone obviously Jewish in a conspiratorial way. I asked as if to imply it's OK to come clean with me. *I'm safe. Can't you tell? I'm a Jew myself.*

"No, I'm a Quaker."

A Quaker? Really? I later met his mother. She was a New York City psychiatrist who looked like Ruth Bader Ginsburg. If she were my mother, I'd be proud of her.

Another chap from Washington, DC, who looks like Jerry Seinfeld, became uncharacteristically tongue-tied when I asked him about it.

The poor Jews of the American South. The lengths they had to go to conceal their identity. Black people couldn't hide their blackness. But being sort of white, we could make up bizarre stories or convert to Quakerism.

Arriving from Chicago and Oxford, where my Jewishness never came up and was never pointed out to me, life in the American South was very different. I was a Jew front and center, a vaudeville act, wherever I appeared.

One friend of mine from the golf club, a big, garrulous guy proud of his "outrageous," roughhouse sense of humor, made loud Jew comments and Jew jokes whenever I was in earshot, and I let them all go, smiling and laughing, waving them off, which may not have been the reaction he expected from me, and eventually, he stopped making them. He was non-PC and made jokes like that to reveal his independent thinking. He made equally derogatory comments about blacks, Asians, Mexicans, and Italians, so he spread his malevolence over every ethnicity. He was good-time Charlie, putting everybody down.

Another friend was at our house one evening with his wife and, as usual, he was smashed within minutes. Our son was being married in Italy later that summer and we were discussing the upcoming nuptials at the Villa San Michele, one of the most beautiful hotels in Florence. I showed the group the suit I was going to wear, which did not meet his approval.

"You're such a cheap Jew," he said.

His wife, my wife, and I, we all said nothing.

"What a cheap Jew," he repeated with a smile.

No protests from the wives.

"Ricky, you are drunk again. Go home," I told him.

It was possible he was trying to talk Jewish jive with me as if he and I were fellow Hebrews, what a laugh, we are all such cheapskates, but it came across badly. He had many chances to rectify or apologize for that episode in the years ahead, and I waited for it, but it never came.

This was a provincial Virginia experience that never happened anywhere else I lived. If his comments were shared in a roomful of closeted Charlottesville Jews, no one would have challenged him, either.

The fact that my wife and his wife stood silent bothered me as much as what he said. I didn't think I'd have to be the one to defend myself at such a moment, but I was wrong about that, too.

In Charlottesville, I always felt like I was being accused of a crime I didn't commit. Only half-Jewish, on my father's side, I wanted to explain, which technically disqualified me from membership according to the Talmud. But they didn't see it that way; they didn't want to hear. I was a Jew. Full stop. And they were right.

Any Jew who wanted to live successfully in a small Southern town had to learn to endure a moderate overhang of anti-Semitism like this, another reason I moved back to Chicago.

Favil David Berns was head of the alumni association of the Marks Nathan Home until his death in 2004, after which no one took over and the alumni association simply disappeared, as every entity and organization eventually does. For fifty-eight years, he maintained the records of the Home, enthusiastically organized alumni gatherings (which my father refused to attend), and was relentlessly upbeat about the Home in general. Without the Marks Nathan Home, Mr. Berns reckoned, he'd be dead, or living under a bridge, his daughter Susan Baron told me. Berns's years in Marks Nathan were happy ones—for him.

All of the records of the Home so faithfully maintained by her lawyer father are now stored in Susan's basement in suburban Glenview, on the site of the former Glenview Naval Air Station. After speaking with her on the telephone, I drove out to meet her, self-conscious in my new Porsche 911S, driving to discuss our orphaned fathers' hard-knock lives. She welcomed me to her immaculate condo with the words "We're family!" She had a plate of delicious cookies for me. I was undone. In Susan I was meeting for the first time another person whose parent had grown up in the orphanage.

The records so assiduously maintained by her father were there for me on Susan's breakfast room table in four large three-ring binders. The Marks Nathan Home was opened May 13, 1906, and closed October 1, 1948. Typical enrollment each year was about three hundred and thirty boys and girls. Approximately fourteen thousand Chicago Jewish children lived in the Home at one time or another.

Those forty-two years of operation and fourteen thousand orphaned lives were now whittled down to four three-ring notebooks stored in a cardboard box in Susan Baron's suburban basement, moved upstairs to her breakfast room that day for my inspection. All those lost lives. I did not know there were so many.

"Susan," I asked her, "do many other people contact you to inquire about the records of the Home?"

"Only two have," she replied. "You and your cousin Gregory."

I was losing it at Susan's house. Only two of us were left to save this history. She offered me a cookie. I'd eat almost all of the cookies by the time I left. In Susan's company, I felt her father's compassion and what the Home could have felt like on its best day, although Susan's new condominium was not exactly South Albany Avenue, and I'd been offered an entire plate of cookies instead of one. All the children who once lived in the Home are now long deceased. However, what of the many thousands of children and grandchildren of these original Home Kids? Where are they? Don't any of them want to know the truth about their parents' or grandparents' lives in the Marks Nathan Home?

On August 30, 1982, Susan Baron's father wrote me the following letter, in response to one of my own:

Mr. Daniel R. Friedman
1835 University Circle
Charlottesville, Virginia 22903

RE: Marks Nathan Jewish Orphan Home
Dear Mr. Friedman:

In reply to your letter of August 4, 1982, regarding any information available concerning your father, Dan Friedman, I am enclosing some materials that I secured from the Jewish Children's Bureau of the Jewish Federation for you, including photocopies of an old publication of *THE ECHO*, where you will find some reference to items authored by your uncles Sol and Irving, your aunt Minna, and your father, Dan.

    I am quite surprised or amazed that your father said his experience was "horrific" and "terrible." My experience in get-togethers with Alumni of all decades generally indicates a contrary opinion. If you have been influenced in that direction by your father, I believe that to be most unfortunate. I hope your opinion changes after you review the materials enclosed.

Best of luck.

                                        Very truly yours,
                                        Favil David Berns

cc: Mr. Aaron Gruenberg

Here I was in 1982 going behind my father's back, writing the head of the alumni group while my father was still alive for details of his life at the Marks Nathan Home, details he wouldn't or couldn't share with me. By this time, I had given up on Dad as a primary source, but I still needed to get to the bottom of his story with or without his cooperation. Dad's story was my story too, and I had a right to it, a right to my history. Of course, I told Dad about my correspondence with Berns, hoping to prod or shame him into response, mentioning Berns's opinion that the Home was a decent place, and that maybe, Dad, you are just a crybaby, but my father only shrugged with disinterest and contempt. I never imagined that thirty-three years after receipt of this letter, I would be eating cookies, going over materials identical to what had been sent to me in 1982, reminiscing in Glenview on the site of an old naval air station with Favil David Berns's daughter, now a widow herself.

I tried throughout my life to free myself from this story line, but it always, always came back to me.

"If you have been influenced in that direction by your father"—only since 1951, dear Mr. Berns, year of my birth, the day I was first introduced to my bold and volatile father, who could ring the scales of the emotional register faster and higher than anyone.

Favil David Berns, I decided, could speak for himself about the Home, and he might be able to speak for some friends, and he gave the Chicago press some remarkable interviews over the years about Home life on the eve of those increasingly rare alumni seders, but he could not speak for my father. No one but my father could speak for him. Contacting Berns had consequences for me. My father thought my communication with him a conspiracy, an act of profound disloyalty. But without Favil David Berns and his daughter Susan, I would have lost all connection with my father's history in the Home.

"They were so poor," Susan told me, shaking her head. "It was sad. It was so sad. Can you imagine? The boys from the Home would follow the ice truck on its rounds and chip off pieces of ice with a screw driver. That was their ice cream."

Mr. Berns's "cc" to Aaron Gruenberg was not lost on me. Who was this Gruenberg? I had asked myself since 1982. In early 2015, I would find out.

The three brief items about my dad in copies of *The Echo* mailed to me by Mr. Berns depict a little boy trapped inside a vast and dark Chicago orphanage circa 1920 and trying mightily to cope with it. The fourth and last item details Dad's only lifetime athletic achievement.

"First day of school, 1921," reads *The Echo*. "Tiny Danny Friedman, 6, sits on the curb, clutching his new scissors and pencil box."

No one will ever take those things away from my dad; they are all he's got.

On the eve of Superintendent Elias Trotzkey's departure from the Home in June 1922, for a three-month "voyage to Europe" to see his mother "before it is too late, perhaps for the last time," some children are lined up and interviewed for *The Echo*:

"Danny Friedman, 7 years—'Misto Twotskey is a good man, because he likes me.'"

Evidently, Dad couldn't enunciate properly but he knew who wielded power inside the Marks Nathan Home and knew he must play up to him.

Trotzkey's nickname among the children was "Daddy." "Daddy," it says in *The Echo*, "is the name he likes best."

Then, in the same year, 1922: "The Juniors have a dramatic group all to themselves. They have a story read to them and then they dramatize it. Every one of the youngsters is given a chance to act. Nathan Segal is in charge and wee little Danny Friedman is his assistant."

In a very few short years, Dad would be the assistant to nobody.

In July 1922, according to *The Echo*, my father distinguished himself in an athletic event. "The small children's three-legged race was the funniest event of the day. The race was won by Dannie Friedman and Esther Bernstein. In this race Esther and Dannie ran without falling, while the others fell once or twice. We wonder how Dannie held her to keep her from falling."

My father and I ran a three-legged race too, throughout my teenage years particularly, and he never let go of me.

This is the extent of my father's published record in the Marks Nathan Home, besides his intake application and discharge paperwork, documents both executed in Jenny's hand.

My little aunt Minna made front page headlines in *The Echo* on two occasions: "Were you one of the lucky ones who was there? If you were, you undoubtedly saw the kissing contest. As Mr. Trotzkey was judge, he had to do the sampling. The winner in this sweet event was Minnie Friedman. We want some boys to volunteer to be judges for a similar contest that will come off in the near future. Don't crowd! For further particulars, see Minnie Friedman."

My poor aunt Minna won a kissing contest with the Home Superintendent, "Daddy," the well-travelled Trotzkey, who "had to do the sampling" in 1922 when Minna was thirteen years old, and had to endure many boys now cued up to kiss her for future kissing contests. She died childless, never reached five feet tall, and lived her lifetime with Jenny as her mother's companion in that apartment on Lake Shore Drive. Minna was a legal secretary who had a long-term affair with her boss, Dad told me, but never married him or anyone else. Gregory and I have fond memories of Minna, who treated us kindly, baked us cookies, and took us to movies in the Loop.

Minna's kissing sequel appeared in the next month's issue of *The Echo*:

> Mr. T. engaged in a kissing duel on the eve of his departure to Europe, when Minnie Friedman presented the children's gift to him after which they kissed. The spectators rapturously applauded. Meanwhile Minnie retreated, but the amorously inclined Rubin intercepted her and tenderly kissed her much to the audience's howling delight. Whereupon our dauntless, aggressive Perry Stern stood up and amicably requested Mr. Rubin to stop. He did quickly. Perry's manner undoubtedly indicated that he yearned for a kiss, too, eh Min?
>
> The kissing scene staged its climax when Miss Lederer presented herself to the front. She was not to be outdone by

the wee charming Minnie so she summoned enough nerve and courage, presented another children's gift to Mr. T. and lo! and behold! They too kissed each other. In all, Mr. T. appeared to be cool and unabashed. Evidently the kissing game is a common much-practiced affair of his.

Kissed repeatedly and in public by the "much-practiced" superintendent of the Home Elias Trotzkey despite attempting retreat, pursued by the amorous Rubin, fondled and kissed by boys following the lead of their beloved Mr. T., all this playing out for years in an orphanage with no father or mother to protect her, it's no wonder little Minna, so beautiful as a child, had that numb, beaten look in middle age and hid away the rest of her days as personal assistant to her imperious, demanding, only-Yiddish-speaking mother. Minna and Jenny lived for twenty years in that two-bedroom apartment, no rugs over the varnished oak floors, very few small pictures hanging from the walls, a sofa and a gray upholstered wingback chair where Jenny sat like a queen. The two of them wore black shrouds. What kind of life was that for Minna in middle age? Why didn't Dad take her in or provide better care for his sister is another legitimate question I'd like to ask, which Dad would never have answered in any case.

At thirteen, an author herself, Minna wrote about fashion and interior decorating for *The Echo's* "Art Number":

> Art does not mean only beautiful pictures exhibited at the Art Institute on Michigan Avenue. Art can be practiced in matters of every day dress and personal appearance, in

choosing house furnishings and decorating rooms. One way of making things artistic is to use colors. There are two kinds of color schemes. There are contrasting colors and analogous colors. Contrasting colors are colors that are exact opposite, such as gray and blue, yellow and brown, old rose and silver. Then there are analogous colors which are different tints and shades of the same color, tan and dark brown, lavender and purple, Alice blue and midnight blue, olive green and grass green.

Now, in the Marks Nathan, which is your home, you have a big opportunity to decorate your rooms according to your idea of what is artistic. Many times in the magazines you will find pictures which would help liven up your Social Room. Why not mount them and hang them up? Then a pretty vase, statue, or any little article of the kind placed in the room to give it a more artistic home-like effect.

It's tragic that Minna, with her refined sensibility, would never live in a place as lovely as the room she imagined as an orphan. She would live with Jenny, who barked at her in Yiddish and German, who neither attempted to learn English nor participate in any aspect of modern American life in Chicago, who never left the apartment unless she had to, who never expressed love to my father or attempted to explain to him the circumstances that required her to move him into the Marks Nathan Home, who never asked his forgiveness, who never, to my knowledge, even kissed him. Jenny came to our house on Apple Tree Lane only once. I remember the occasion of it, her slowly getting out of Dad's black Cadillac in our circular drive, my pretty mother's dread at her arrival. My grandmother, a large, slow-moving, once-dangerous bird of prey, was dressed, as was her custom, for a funeral in the old country, all in black—black housedress, black wool stockings even on that warm summer day, and black lace-up shoes. Minna was the same, all in black, but half the size, following her stooped mother up the driveway to our house like a pair in mourning.

Dad and his sister Minna were little victims of the Marks Nathan Home because of their age, size, and vulnerability. My uncles Irving and Si were mid-sized victims. In all the editions of *The Echo* I could obtain from Susan Baron, her father, and the Jewish Federation, Irving and Si were mentioned only a couple of times. Irv—a quiet and bookish lawyer who lived down the street from us in Glencoe in a split-level house on Forest Way Drive, father of Mark and Richard, my beloved and brilliant cousins and playmates whose lives have been filled with extraordinary accomplishment, nearly my brothers, my friends throughout my lifetime—was cited for his superior grades at Polk school and participation in the Home's Art Club. I was always comfortable and warmly welcomed at Irving's home, an easy bicycle ride from Apple Tree Lane. I felt loved by him. Irv looked at me with tenderness, as if I were his son, and I spent a lot of time in Forest Way Drive with my lively, unpredictable Friedman cousins. In our high school years, their Glencoe home became the scene of our extraordinary recreational drug experimentation circa 1969. Lots of pot, mescaline, and LSD were consumed in Aunt Mary's kitchen by five or six utter fools who somehow survived it all, but barely.

My entirely mute, almost shell-shocked uncle Simon, who lived eleven years in the Marks Nathan Home, longer than any of his siblings, probably because he was the most uncomplaining, earned praise in *The Echo* for singing "like a nightingale" in a Home musical event. Si spoke in whispers, would sell carpeting at Sears, and had a scholar's passion for his coin collection, the prize of which was a rare 1955 "doubled-die" penny, which he displayed to my father and me with pride. Si created a line of individual Lucite coin display cases which he hoped to produce and sell to other collectors, but never got anywhere with this project although Lucite display cases for collectible coins became the industry standard. Si's son, Glenn, was my contemporary, too, although we never saw much of each other. Our family lived on the North Shore and Si never left the old neighborhood on the South Side, but I remember how Dad and I would meet Si in the Loop under the L tracks for lunch at the Blackhawk, Si looking beaten, hunched over in his London Fog, looking up at Dad and smiling with real affection. I had more in common with my Glencoe Friedman cousins, all of whom attended New Trier, the great anti–Marks Nathan Home. Glenn had a son, another Dan Friedman, another Kasiel Skolnick look-alike bristling with energy and intelligence, who would become the father of five.

Dad had a second sister, the beautiful Annette, whose heart condition prevented her from moving into Marks Nathan. Annette lived with Jenny until she married Rudy Cooper and predeceased her mother by twenty years. Annette's granddaughter is my equally beautiful second cousin Lynne Weinstein Reisner, who I knew as a child and know again today. Lynne's father, Jerry Weinstein, was a noted Chicago mensch, accomplished athlete, man-about-town, and the owner of the famous Oak Street boutique, Ultimo, the preferred shopping venue for style mavens Saul Bellow and Allan Bloom, who would come in together on certain Saturday afternoons. Bellow noted those shopping expeditions to Ultimo in *Ravelstein,* all part of our Chicago landscape and lore.

Jews are supposed to be so funny but my Jews were not. I could only be so funny myself, carrying the burden of my father's Home years and trying to make sense of it. After their long childhood in the Home, Irv and Si needed to be very quiet the rest of their lives, Irv shut off in his bedroom with a pile of papers and magazines, Si lost in his coin collection, depleting all their energy during their boyhoods coping with the full-on hardship of Marks Nathan. To me, even as a boy, it was plain that Marks Nathan sucked the juice from them. My father loved his brothers and Minna, and treated them with patience and care, unlike the contempt with which Dad treated the rest of the world. He knew they were badly, irretrievably broken by the Home. He knew he was badly damaged by the Home, too, but the Home did not break Dad or extinguish his fire. Somehow, by some weird twist of luck, some extraordinary resilience particular to him, Marks Nathan only inflamed and magnified Dad's fury. Dad one day was going to stand atop the rubble of the Marks Nathan Home with a sword, for himself and his siblings, despite his mother and father, and pound his chest for the world to see him having come through.

Among my uncles, Sol, the eldest, was the giant. In a section called "Personal Hobbies," Sol writes in *The Echo* in 1921, age fifteen, what matters to him most: "Reading great books, playing indoor baseball, playing chess, arguing with Emmanuel Slotnick, writing stories, having work I enjoy."

Unlike the others, Sol was unfazed by Home life. In fact, he ruled the place. Sol was born smart and positive. He extracted the good from the Home and floated above the rest. Perhaps Sol thought the only way to save his siblings was to set the highest example for them. They could watch their older brother thrive and learn from example. I know my father studied him carefully, missing nothing. Sol was King of the Home Kids, the success of Marks Nathan. He was Head Boy, editorial writer and historian, wit and raconteur, Home cantor, admired by supervisors and kids, and loved and needed by his little brother, my father, his junior by eight years. Sol was my father's beacon. Dad knew that if anyone was going to get him out of this mess, it would be Sol, and Dad was right.

Sol left a long paper trail in *The Echo*.

"We have two new papers published at the Home," the omniscient narrator of *The Echo*, faculty supervisor Mr. Blumenthal, writes. "Sollie Friedman is editor of one, which he calls 'The Magazine Record.' It contains a brief summary or digest of all national magazines published that month." This is the work of my fifteen-year-old uncle, Gregory's dad, in 1921. The real *Reader's Digest* did not appear until 1922.

"Sol Friedman furnished the Editorial Room with a bookcase and writing table, chairs . . . and lovely pictures which adorn the walls."

Sollie wrote poetry, Home humor, Home gossip, and embodied "Home Spirit." He published his own paper within *The Echo* called *The Free Press*. "We the editors of this paper," Sol wrote, "will do our best to make this a Free Press and we will publish Free Speech, and your grudges if you have any."

Sol, too, wrote for the big "Arts Number":

"Art is the second language of the business world as well as that of the universe; but art is a more beautiful language than business since all nations understand it."

He wrote short biographies of Jewish artists—Jozef Israëls, Max Liebermann, Lesser Ury, Ernst Oppler, Jeff Oppenheimer, Eugene Spiro, Ernst Josephson, and Camille Pissarro. Sol also considered the Jews' place in world history, in his own words:

"Such a race is a powerful race composed of people who are faithful to themselves as well as to God. No nation, no matter how powerful, will succeed in wiping out the people of Israel, for they are still guided, as they were in the days of old, by the watchful hand of God."

In every way, Greg is the image of Sol, his dynamic and loving father. When I'm with Greg now and look into his face, it's not a stretch to say we are Dan and Sol together again, the way they were as boys.

The Marks Nathan Home was a serious place. It was the first Orthodox Jewish orphanage built in the city of Chicago. The Orthodox Jews newly arrived in the city, fleeing miserable shtetls like Knyszyn at the turn of the century, found American Jewry under command of the German Reform Jews, who, they believed, had watered down the faith in favor of Americanization and mediocrity. The Eastern Jews were shocked to find their German brethren so secular and removed from the values of their shared religion. "Deep down in their hearts they are *goyim*" was the Orthodox sentiment, so the Eastern Jews created their own hospitals, schools, and orphanages. The anguish of submitting to the charity of the Reform Jews was too much for some Orthodox Jews. They would rather have died in the street than accept the "strange and un-Jewish" practices of the Reformed institutions. In the minds of the Orthodox, the established Reform Jews in Chicago were a menace to their faith.

In 1913, in the Annual Report for the Jewish Federation, the Chicago board that oversaw the orphanage, Trotzkey wrote: "My greatest ambition is to see that our children grow up to be good Jews, not simply Jews, but Jews that know all about Judaism, Jews with Jewish thoughts and Jewish hearts. I am not satisfied with Sunday School Jews. I will bring all my energies to bear on the fact that our children should learn and know Judaism. In the school everything is taught in English, but I hope that in time our Hebrew School will be the model for all Chicago."

This meant that life inside the Marks Nathan Home was demanding and rigorous for the small people who lived there. The Home kids were required to attend six hours of Hebrew classes per week. The Torah was recited and committed to memory, prayers were spoken aloud in Hebrew in the Home's own synagogue every morning for fifteen minutes, grace was said before and after every meal, only kosher food was served, and the boys were required to wear yarmulkes at all meals and carry them in their pockets at all times.

As important as any of its teachings, children in the Home were warned of "intermarriage evil." The Orthodox Jews did not permit their children to marry non-Jews. For the Orthodox, marrying outside the faith was a cardinal sin. Reformed Jews intermarried at a rate that horrified the newly arrived Orthodox. Christians weren't happy about intermarriage, either. Basically, everyone was unhappy when a Jew married a Christian, except maybe the couple themselves, at least for a few brief years before ancient hatreds kicked in. Today, many Reform rabbis routinely conduct interfaith marriages, but it took half a century to get there.

The Orthodox curriculum of the Home passed over the head of my father, the son of a man who had already begun the Reform process by changing his name. Dad's Orthodox education, he told me, turned him against all Orthodoxy. Orthodoxy led to wars and bloodshed, he believed from the bottom of his heart. Dad did not want to live like a Jew in Knyszyn. He did not want to live in a tribe. He wanted to rule Chicago, live independently, answer to no ancient system, etiquette, or decree. Although fluent, Dad spoke Yiddish only once in a while—it wasn't modern. Dad refused to attend temple or practice Judaism throughout his life—it wasn't American. Dad married a *shiksa* because he hated his mother. Dad never renounced Judaism; he was a Jew, whatever that meant, and like him, I was a Jew, too. Dad chose to leave Judaism alone in the room with me as just another huge, emotionally-laden subject he refused to talk about or explain.

Dad expressed himself as Jewish by worshipping Sandy Koufax, loving deli food, and buying Israel bonds during the Six-Day War, which I watched being sold door-to-door with amazing success to every homeowner on Apple Tree Lane. Our neighbors in Glencoe outdid themselves in their love of Israel during those tense weeks of June and July 1967, when they rallied together, making our new North Shore subdivision feel like a ghetto in the Pale or the Southwest Side.

As for me, I knew fifteen or twenty colorful words and phrases in Yiddish with which I peppered my speech, to the amusement of some friends. Ours was the only house in a completely Jewish neighborhood with a Christmas tree. My mother took me to mass at Faith, Hope and Charity Catholic Church, and I never once stepped inside Hebrew School. My mother told me straight to my face that I wasn't Jewish and that she did not want me to be a Jew. Dad really did not care one way or another. He'd let me figure that out for myself, a puzzle so complicated and nuanced I needed all the help I could find. Thanks for nothing, Dad. I was the only kid on Apple Tree Lane to attend school over the Jewish Holidays. "Friedman?" my first grade teacher Mrs. Grieger asked me. "What are you doing here?" I was in first grade. I didn't know the answer. Besides me, Bob and Bill, the two school janitors, and two Irish kids, the entire school grades K–6 was completely empty because West School was built to accommodate the new, exclusively Jewish subdivisions on Glencoe's new West Side. In Glencoe, I was a resident alien, a half-Jew, on the wrong side, my father's, living among the Jews and loving everything about them, their food, their storytelling and free association, their guts and fearless *chutzpah*.

By marrying a Catholic Croatian, however beautiful, and by refusing to discuss Judaism, Dad confused me about where I belonged, my heritage, my religious identity, the whole package. Who was I? Jew or Gentile? And what was I supposed to do about that? Rather late in life, after both my parents were dead with these questions never resolved or even properly addressed, a Catholic priest finally shed light on the matter by telling me that Judaism and Catholicism were "a beautiful complement," and that satisfied me at the moment. That priest, Jozo Grbes, now a crony of Chicago Archbishop Blase Cupich, was at the time head of St. Jerome Croatian Catholic Church on South Princeton Avenue, where my immigrant Croatian grandparents met and were married, and where my mother was baptized and attended elementary school. Jozo Grbes showed me proof that my father attended St. Jerome with my mother. In Sunday church programs from the 1950s, my father advertised his paper business, Associated Salvage Company. Spectacular Kasiel Skolnick–type move for a boy from the Orthodox Marks Nathan Home, iconoclastic, so typical of my freewheeling father, and an act of love because he adored my mother in those days. Their intermarriage worked, for a while, until I was born; then they tried to figure out how to raise me and failed.

I was a Jew and a Catholic. I didn't know what to do about it, and no one gave me a road map. Choosing between the two was choosing between my parents, making me decide whom I loved more. For certain, I couldn't be two things at once. I had to be one. When people asked what I was I needed a one-word answer.

The reconciliation of "conflicting and multiple identities," as Irène Némirovsky wrote, became the story of my life, the tangled web I could not escape. At or around this moment, when my sense of self was emerging, when I looked around the world trying to figure out where I fit in, I slowly recognized that I did not fit in anywhere but mongrel dog Chicago, an entire city of immigrants and half-breeds. I felt comfortable in Chicago among millions of others wrestling with the same dilemma. Knowing who you are and where you come from is the work of a lifetime.

My father received care packages in the Marks Nathan Home from a Chicago family named Freund. If the Freunds had so much extra food they could give some away, my father reasoned at the time, then they must be rich, and rich was good. My father was grateful to the Freunds and told me he considered changing his name from Friedman to Freund to be like them, an easier move, after all, than going from Skolnick to Friedman. I considered this, and it made me uneasy. At what point do you stop with the name changing? I have never met a Freund in Chicago but if I do, I will give them belated thanks for giving my father hope. All this taught me: you weren't really one person. You could be many people in one lifetime, and I found this freeing but destabilizing.

"Dad, why did you marry a non-Jew?"

"Because I hated my mother!"

"Mom, why did you marry Dad?"

"I don't know. I found him dashing. He was funny."

With such stellar reasoning, my parents married and condemned me to a life in goydom among the Jews and the ghetto among the Gentiles. I didn't know anyone else like me in this conflicted space except my brother and my cousins Gregory, Mark, and Richard, because Sol and Irving married *shiksas,* too. Along with Dad, Sol and Irv both dove headlong into the murky waters of intermarriage evil. According to the Orthodox thinkers who raised the Friedman children in the Marks Nathan Home, intermarriage was assimilation, abandonment of the faith, but it was the quickest route to Americanization, and America won out, that's how I figured it.

We all (sort of) worked out our own solutions to the mixed-marriage conundrum. I suffered through it the most, thinking I was Jewish one day and Catholic the next, then, finally, both. My brother considered himself a Jew but married a non-Jew, had no religious education, did not attend temple, and did not require his children to attend temple. Richard married a Jew and raised his two sons as Jews. Mark was a political activist, extremely spiritual but not religious, and moved to San Francisco where he could be (and was) anything he wanted to be (including Mayor of El Cerrito in the East Bay). Gregory went to Hebrew school for one day, then told his father that he refused to ever go again. His dad, Sol, cantor of the Marks Nathan Home, agreed. Plus, it had become a logistic hassle to get Gregory to Hebrew School since the family had moved to Crystal Lake by that time, thirty-five miles from the school on Vernon Avenue in Glencoe. Greg married a non-Jew, then remarried her. I married a non-Jew, had three children with her, divorced her, then married yet another *shiksa*, which could be the title for another book.

———

It was 1945. My father was just honorably discharged from the United States Army, spending the war years working a desk job at Fort Benning, Georgia. He was back in Chicago now, working for his uncle, the famous Max Patinkin, founder of Peoples Iron and Metal, at 5835 S. Loomis Street, and somehow got his hands on a mile-long, black, four-door 1941 Cadillac with black convertible top, one of the most elegant cars ever made in America. He was driving it to work on a Monday morning on Western Avenue when he saw a stunning blonde waiting at a bus stop. Kasiel Skolnick's DNA kicked in, the very DNA still working its magic within me, thank god. He slammed on the brakes, put the Caddy into reverse, and got the blonde in the car.

"And Danny, that's how I met your mother."

———

The first Marks Nathan Home building (converted to a luxury single-family home that sold for $3.5 million in 2013 to a handsome young couple photographed in the *Tribune*, the building's history as an orphanage reduced to a mere footnote) was on North Wood Street in the now hip Wicker Park neighborhood. It opened May 13, 1906, with twenty-nine orphans. Soon afterwards, it was decided that a much larger facility was needed, so the Home relocated to 1550 South Albany Avenue, opening November 17, 1912, with 186 orphaned children. By the time Dad moved in on February 25, 1920, the Marks Nathan Home had 341 "Home Kids" admonished in *The Echo* to improve their lives and environment.

The Echo's editorial mission was to cheer and uplift the Home Kids with corny jokes and news, and to educate them about physical and mental health, meals, manners, Home economy, self-improvement, and the importance of remaining cheerful despite the awful confusion and realities of their young lives. Its student writers had dreams of making it "the greatest orphan home newspaper in America." Every edition was filled with instruction and words of inspiration.

"Reading develops the mind," one issue stated. "Start now and read the best of books." My father and his brothers were lifetime readers of history, biography, and serious literature.

Student health was another frequent topic: "Flies spread disease. Swat them before they get you."

Most of *The Echo* was high-minded; all of it was practical and well-intended. It shed light on just how tough it was to run a large Chicago orphanage in the early 1920s. Under Mr. Blumenthal's supervision, the Home newspaper published a highly sanitized version of events.

"Good manners—show them at each meal. It costs nothing. Remember one is impressed a great deal by one's manners."

My father was the fastest eater I'd ever seen. I'd watch my father eat and began to eat that way myself, faster even than him, as if in some sort of competition. Apparently, at mealtimes, kids would engage in a grabbing match for the best pieces of food and the slow kids got stuck with the worst, or an empty bowl. Elegant manners were nowhere to be seen. Mealtime was survival of the fittest.

"Relax, Dad," I'd tease him from across the kitchen table in Glencoe. "You're not in the Home anymore. They are not going to take it away from you."

And he would laugh.

The Home employed no janitors or grounds staff to clean up after the children.

"Pick up all rubbish. Make the Home more beautiful than you found it."

Dad did not get this one, either. His bedroom was a mess, the curtains were always drawn, his clothes piled up on the floor.

Student mental health in the Home was a continual worry.

"Whistle—Whistle away the 'blues.' Don't let worry, sadness or anxiety attack you. Whistle when despondent or unhappy. Whistle, get happy again. Be gay and merry—whistle!"

This acknowledgement of sadness and anxiety in the Marks Nathan population was written before psychotherapy and the universal medication of children and adolescents for depression.

"Boys and girls can help save money by preventing waste," one issue implored. "One of the best ways is by saving electric lights. Never allow a large globe to burn all night. Make sure there is one small globe to burn all night in the washrooms. If you are the last one in the tank, turn off the lights when you leave. Little boys and little girls should also see that the lights are off when they leave the playroom. Bulbs cost a great deal of money. They burn out quickly. Electricity is made from coal and costs a great deal of money. The Home spent $243 in March and in April $233. Help cut this in half."

Making the children aware of Home economy was important, but the goal of cutting the utility bill in half during a Chicago winter may not have been practical.

"We must eat right, chew our food slowly and digest it properly, exercise enough, sleep well, have a sufficient amount of fresh air to keep fit. Be natural in your living. Don't go to extremes. Bear in mind that health is not a thing to be trifled with."

Dad always went to extremes and never exercised save for walking around Apple Tree Lane smoking a Parliament with Hy Spector. He took up golf late in life, always riding around in an electric cart, driving up to his ball as closely as possible, taking a swing, then walking two steps back into the cart.

"Many people are surprised to find their hair falling out rapidly. Keep your scalp and hair very clean. Shampoo your hair at least once a week with warm water and Ivory or Fairy. Exposing hair to sunlight should be encouraged. Sunlight is destructive to disease germs and will keep the hair in fine condition."

Rapid hair loss in children, especially in an orphan home, was caused by sudden or severe stress, such as the loss of a parent. These kids in the Marks Nathan Home were losing their hair because they were traumatized, not because of insufficient sunlight or poor hygiene.

A nine-year-old girl named Rose Slotnick wrote:

"A smile will win you friends. It will do more than that; it will change a foe to a friend. Keep on the sunny side of life. There is nothing that happens, but it might have been worse. Everything will be all right if you believe it to be so. No matter what happens, keep a sunny disposition and the world will think so much more of you."

These healthy admonishments had no impact on Dad, who during his early years in the Home could not even read. Dad wasn't cheerful or sunny as an adult; he was suspicious, and he never whistled. He wept at Puccini and loved the novels of Bellow, particularly the early ones. Bellow was his man who spoke his highest truth and *The Adventures of Augie March* was his story. He took my mother to Milan to attend a performance of *Aida*. He loved Sid Caesar, Woody Allen, Lenny Bernstein, and Lenny Bruce, and not much else, except me. His outlook was bleak and fatalistic; he believed that chaos was the natural state of man and that civilization was on the brink of implosion; he did not believe in God. He'd tell me all this, in staccato shorthand, from his black Eames lounge chair in his bedroom, surrounded by piles of books and newspapers, where he experienced a few rare moments of relaxed reflection.

Anger was his defining characteristic. He was angry all the time with everyone except me. Anger was the great fuel that blew us out of the West Side. Anger was the emotion he mastered, that propelled him above and beyond his starting point at the Marks Nathan Home. Dad believed it was the single power that most improved our lives. It was never a surprise to me that fatherless basketball players became NBA All-Stars.

These older, better-adjusted kids editorializing for *The Echo*, the city's future judges, journalists, and business leaders, were working desperately hard to improve themselves and be positive, but in 1915, the year of Dad's birth, Chicago was a violent city of race war and tragedy. In 1915, the SS *Eastland* rolled on its side while docked on the Chicago River at Clark Street and 844 passengers and crew were drowned. My father was admitted to the Home in February, 1920, six months after the 1919 Chicago race riots, the worst race rioting in the history of Illinois. This was as low as you could go in Chicago or anywhere in the world. His father was dead, he had just been placed in an orphanage after reaching the minimum enrollment age, his mother was penniless with six children and could not pay the $40 per child per month fee the Home asked of her and then waived.

On certain Sundays, Jenny in her black shroud and wide-brimmed black hat would bring a packed lunch and visit her five children at the Home. If the weather allowed, they'd play together as a family in Douglas Park across the street from the main entrance. I have a photograph of one such sorry visit, the siblings lined up, my dad looking five or six, Sol towering over them all, nearly Jenny's height, already a man in a belted black jacket and knickers, possibly fifteen. Adorable Minna with her beaming smile in an unlaundered, unpressed white dress, her black bangs chopped and mangled. Irving and Si trying to be good boys and look at the camera in their dingy shirts hastily tucked in for this rare event—a family photograph! The trees of Douglas Park are leafless, black, and stunted. This photo could be early spring 1920 or 1921. My father, the midget of this impoverished family unit standing in this barren deathly landscape, looks disturbed, distracted, sharp eyes averted from the camera, in a filthy shirt, his huge intelligent head on his tiny torso, his body caught twisting to get away, not squarely facing the camera like the rest of them. The best you can say of Jenny is that she was there; at least on that occasion she showed up.

When I first saw this photograph—the only family photograph from my father's six years in the Marks Nathan Home—I was sickened and wept. Immediately I saw it was true. This photograph was proof that everything he could and could not tell me about his years in the Home was completely true. The Home was a nightmare, the depths of which I could never comprehend. It was worse, far worse for him, than he had let on. That was why he didn't talk. That was why he wept whenever I asked him about it. Age did not mellow him; distance and worldly success did not soften his attitude. He never considered the Marks Nathan Home as if it were an object, picking it up, turning it around in his hand to examine it from another angle, as you would a glass globe or orb, a shell or rock, something curious out of nature you might find at the beach or in the mountains. I wanted Dad to reevaluate, to come to terms, to soften just a little, to step outside or above it and look at it from a different angle. But he couldn't do that. And he failed both of us in that way. I wanted to see him grow and get past it. I knew the only way for him to get past it was to tell the whole truth about it, to me, his eldest son, because I was the only one he could tell it to, because I knew I could take it all, however awful. *Dad, please tell me, talk to me about it, it can't be that bad. Dad, I am your son, please just tell me.*

Three

Rue des Beaux-Arts

In 2011, in the second half of the year, I lived in Oxford, England, city of my alma mater, where I escaped to sort out my exit strategy after a long marriage, to meditate in pubs, to write in the Radcliffe Camera, and to contemplate the disaster that had just befallen me. I'm still not certain I survived it. Divorce is an incredibly violent thing to happen to you. Oxford was my safe haven, a familiar place to regroup. I needed to begin a new life in a new setting. In some idealized way, I thought, I could move back to my university city in Great Britain and grow old there among its libraries, bookstores, and gardens.

My parents visited me in Oxford during my student years only once, in 1974, during the depths of the energy crisis. They came from Chicago over the Christmas holidays, and the ancient city was cold and black as night by 3:00 p.m. My mother wore a full-length, white mink coat for that visit and stood out, as only a gorgeous Chicago broad could, among the fastidious dons and their threadbare wives. We had an invitation one evening to Richard and Mary Ellmann's house, Iris Murdoch and John Bayley were in attendance, and Larzer Ziff, and I am ashamed to admit I wished my mother had dressed with greater discretion among those scholars that evening. Beneath the white mink was a tight Pucci minidress and white go-go boots. She looked fabulous—in Chicago, not in Oxford—and I was ass enough to tell her so. But she would not tolerate my newly acquired Oxford snobbism. Not for a second would her fashion sense be called into question. She was from Back of the Yards and could handle any situation from far tougher customers than Richard Ellmann and me. I was her completely inexperienced son, and she and Dad were paying my way to this fancy place. Show me the respect I deserve.

"James Joyce is shit if you don't know how to deal with people," she said, and would not speak to me the rest of the trip. She was right about me then. My mother was about the furthest thing from my mind when she came to visit in 1974.

Dad ignored our dispute. He floated above it.

"The wheel is always turning," he liked to say. Today's downtrodden are tomorrow's champions. To have his son at Oxford was proof.

The graduate of the Marks Nathan Home took it all in. His nostrils flared as he walked the city flagstones. He looked at me with eyes wide, speechless. The veteran of South Albany Avenue knew where his namesake had landed. He could not help but be delighted and proud. He had contributed mightily to my achievement and reveled in it. Without him, I could not have done it. The fact is, I wanted both of them to be proud of me, but only one was, Dad. Mom was a glamour girl. The bookish life in Oxford held little appeal.

My first new friend in Oxford upon my return was Nighat Malik, the housing director of my college, Worcester, who controlled the keys to dozens of centrally located houses and flats, and with Nighat on my side I always had a roof over my head. Accommodations in Oxford have always been scarce. Nighat and I had been communicating via email. She wrote: "Just come. We will have something for you." Based on that assurance alone I booked a ticket and arrived at Worcester, not knowing where I was going to sleep that early September evening.

For two months she set me up in a tiny college house down in Jericho on Nelson Street, which backed up to the Worcester athletic fields and gardens, before moving me to a four-hundred-square-foot basement flat on Worcester Place, just off Walton Street, Senator Bill Bradley's favorite place to stay, she told me. I was aware of occupying the great man's digs, decorated with a few of his personal effects. Other great men visited or stayed nearby. I saw Salman Rushdie, a fatwa hanging over him, once or twice a week shopping in the Covered Market, Julian Barnes having dinner in the Standard on Walton Street, and Martin Amis browsing shop windows on the Turl. I felt like I knew those guys well enough I could almost speak to them. I attended student poetry readings, rode a bicycle everywhere, played basketball in the Iffley Road gym. Every person next to me in the pub or café was writing a book.

During those happy months I dated a woman I met on a website called Blues Match, accessible only to the graduates of Oxford and Cambridge. Blues Match was a wildly successful dating service. It hinted at academic achievement and exclusivity and was built on the premise that you would very likely want to shag someone you went to university with. I met at least two otherwise demure English women who claimed they intended "to shag their entire way through Blues Match." This was fertile territory for a guy like me who had arrived in Oxford with no female companion.

Ex-*Financial Times*, a sophisticated, pukka, plummy-voiced blonde and near contemporary of mine at Lady Margaret Hall, she lived in a cheerful row house in a smart London backwater around the corner from the Blue Boar pub, near Richmond Park, and under the busy flight path into Heathrow where the planes come in low and slow. She thought I lived in bohemian squalor in Oxford, which I did, and relished, and would not stay with me overnight. That meant that every Friday after 5:00 p.m. I became a so-called Senior Night Rider and bought a bus ticket at the old age pensioner's discounted rate to Shepherd's Bush. At "the Bush," I'd take the 283 or the 72 past Hammersmith to the Blue Boar and walk less than one hundred meters to her tidy house. Door to door, two hours. She always rewarded me in the front hall with a long kiss.

We laughed. We ate and drank. We talked endlessly about our children and our childhoods. We walked her little dogs in Richmond Park, giving wide berth to the rutting stags. We went to the cinema, the Chelsea Arts Club, and browsed the London galleries. We saw Antony Sher in Arthur Miller's *Broken Glass* and Sharon Gless in Jane Juska's *A Round-Heeled Woman*. We had late dinners at Ronnie Scott's. We attended dinner parties with her attractive and accomplished friends. Our British American confluence was aphrodisiac, the cultural fireworks surprising and exotic. I bought her an embroidered pillow at a gift shop around the corner: "Nobody Does It Better." We began to talk about me moving in with her, becoming her "lodger."

Yet when I returned to Oxford Sunday night after every busy weekend in London, something in me exhaled. I decompressed as the big red double-decker came down Headington Hill towards Oxford center. Somehow, even at that late hour, the Old Bookbinders pub down by the canal in Jericho was still going strong, open mic night and the place was throbbing. The singing, storytelling, and recitation of free verse made me happier than all London's cavalcade of status and vanity and fine people.

Starting a new life with a new woman, I discovered, finding a new place to start over, was not so simple after all. I did not know whom to consult on the subject or where to go. I couldn't talk to my dad about it because he'd been dead for twenty-five years. He'd have no special insight anyway. His generation suffered through miserable marriages until the bitter end. I was entirely on my own. Could I make a home in Oxford where I graduated from university decades earlier? Could I move to Paris, where I worked as a journalist for sixteen years? What about Dalmatia, where I had been visiting every summer, where I had a family village outside Split and nearly one hundred cousins on my mother's side? Nat, Peachie, and Victoria, my children, all married, lived in San Francisco, Southern California, and Brooklyn. I would not, could not, live near them, become an accessory, and cramp their style.

She and I took a weekend together to Paris as my time in Oxford was winding down, and I found the surprise answer there during the last week of November over Thanksgiving, the city empty of tourists, mists rising from the river, stick-figure pedestrians' black silhouettes against the gray sky painted by Albert Marquet or André Derain. Christmas decorations were beginning to appear, evergreen trees spray-painted bright silver, even, outrageously, brilliant gold, for sale outside the smart shops in the Carré des Antiquaires.

When we arrived at my beloved Rue des Beaux-Arts, we were shown a small, elegantly appointed room at the rear of the building. By now a veteran of scaled-down accommodations on Nelson Street and Worcester Place, training ground for my future as a newly single man, the room suited me just fine.

She immediately made noises. The Left Bank was clearly not the George V.

"This room's too small," she snapped at me. "It's entirely unacceptable."

My father was raised in the Marks Nathan Home on the Wrong Side of Chicago. Thanks to him, there was much in life I didn't need, including the most luxurious hotel room in Paris. But I ran downstairs to the front desk and fortunately a bigger, more impressive room overlooking the street was available. The upgrade cost an additional €100 per night and I was relieved to pay to keep her happy, at least for those last few days.

Looking at Van Gogh's *Bedroom in Arles* in the Musée d'Orsay, I told her, dead serious, I must be completely plain with her, that's how I want to live. She looked at me in utter disbelief. I must be joking. But I was not. That's precisely how I want to live. She and I weren't exactly on the same page.

The next morning, we walked across the river to the Grand Palais to view a major show of the collected works of Gertrude Stein and her brothers Leo and Michael, who amassed one of the greatest art collections of the twentieth century and who were nothing less than the Medicis or Borgias of their time. The Steins' staggering hoard of masterworks fills the entire museum. Among the famous paintings, sculpture, and photographs is a large and detailed architectural model by Le Corbusier for a house commissioned by the Steins and built in the Paris suburbs in 1927.

This exquisite model of the Villa Stein suddenly brought to life for me the glass and steel Mies van der Rohe towers on Lake Shore Drive in Chicago, which I had not seen in over thirty years. A bulb went off amid the fashionable mob, a ray of sunshine. Standing there in the Grand Palais, in the press of people, I had a warm feeling and hope about the Mies towers in the city of my birth. "Less is more," Mies said. My thinking exactly. Those towers might be a wonderful place for me. Maybe I could live there.

Two days later I was back at my desk in Oxford, in the Radcliffe Camera, now communicating with a real estate agent in Chicago who specialized in the sale of apartments in Mies's landmark towers at 860-880 North Lake Shore Drive. It turned out, miraculously, even financially dismembered by divorce, that I could afford one. If I didn't act on this convergence of illuminations, I thought, I would act on nothing.

The towers at 860-880 were completed in 1951, the year of my birth, and they became an immediate sensation. My father and mother drove me from Glencoe in the back seat of one of Dad's Coupe de Villes to take a close look at them. It's noteworthy we went at all. My parents had long since given up on the idea of living in Chicago; white flight was in high gear; our future was Glencoe and the North Shore. Dad parked on Chestnut, or Delaware, or Lake Shore Drive, shut off the motor, and gazed up at the buildings that were already being called "The Glass Houses." I'm certain we made this expedition after the *Life* magazine homage to Mies, "Emergence of a Master Architect," a photographic essay by Frank Scherschel. My dad paused longer than usual before stating his opinion of the place:

"No privacy. Couldn't live here."

"Dad, you're wrong," I thought. "Those buildings are beautiful."

More than half a century after that drive-by with Mom and Dad, I moved in.

The architect I hired to gut and remodel my new Chicago home was Vladimir Radutny, a Ukrainian Jew whose personal story mirrored mine. He arrived in the United States in 1988 as a seven-year-old with his parents, four suitcases, and two hundred dollars. He shared my fascination with Mies, and working with him—another Chicago immigrant like the rest of us—completed the circle of my return to the city of my birth.

After many years of uncertainty, moving from place to place, and alone, I pledged that I would stay here forever. My search, after leaving Virginia, took a very long time, but finally I was home again.

Four

Home Kids—Two

Of the six boys' and girls' dormitories in Marks Nathan, one was set aside for bed-wetters. It was in this dorm that my father lived his entire six-plus years. While the Home was progressive academically, and saw to the intellectual needs of its bright Jewish children, around bed-wetting it was not. The treatment of bed-wetting was Stone Age. Supervisors believed the large number of bed-wetters in the Home could be shamed into stopping. They forced the bed-wetter's face down into his urine-soaked sheets and held it there. Then the wet sheets were hung out to dry on the iron railing above the bed for all to see. A generation later treatment for bed-wetting had not much improved. My father had his face held down into his wet sheets every morning by a supervisor in the Home, and he half-heartedly held my face into the soaked sheets on Apple Tree Lane at least once ("Don't hold it against me Danny! I don't know how to be a father.")

When I was ten, my pediatrician recommended complete anesthesia and the insertion of a catheter through the urethra to make sure my bladder was not too small (it was not). I quit wetting the bed like I quit smoking cigarettes—one day I just stopped, but wetting, soaking, the bed daily was my first red flag that life on earth would not be perfect. Two of my children, to their dismay, also wet the bed, but by this time I knew it came with the territory of being a Friedman. I'm sure Kasiel Skolnick wet the bed, as well. Now, experts claim, there is a gene for bed-wetting. According to the Mayo Clinic, "if one or both of a child's parents wet the bed . . . their child has a significant chance of wetting the bed, too." We had an aptitude for math, loved the English language, and we wet the bed.

The children in the Home attended public school and returned to the Home for Hebrew lessons five days a week followed by homework.

The boys in Marks Nathan played sports and had teams, but the Home had no athletic facilities or playground besides barren Douglas Park across the street. Recreation for the Home Kids took place on the sidewalk or indoors. Trotzkey admitted in one of his Annual Reports that "our children are street children under the influence of the street . . . our home is a large ghetto home."

Chess was popular among these brainy Jewish boys, and the chess team at the Marks Nathan Home was a big deal. My father and his brothers played throughout their lives, with an improvisational, attacking style, generally winning within a dozen moves or less, using a classic Ruy Lopez opening, or a four pawns attack, and an impregnable Alekhine defense, which they had mastered after playing thousands of games against hyper-competitive kids in the Home playroom. Playing with Dad, I learned if I could withstand the fireworks of his much-practiced opening salvo and get him into the mid-game, I'd stand a chance of winning, but this never happened. At best, I might get him off balance and make him focus, but I never beat him. With no playground and surrounded by the mean streets of the Southwest Side, it's no wonder chess was so popular among the boys.

The Lawndale neighborhood surrounding the Home could be dangerous and violent. The Home Kids had to fight their way to and from Polk Elementary School, another dreary brick monstrosity two very long city blocks south. Larger groups of non-Jewish kids made the walk to school miserable. The fights got desperate. One Home Kid brought a revolver to one of these brawls. Instead of shooting somebody, he fired it over the heads of the antagonists, scattering them.

One of the heroes of the Home Kids was the boxer Barney Ross, born Dov-Ber Rasofsky, who witnessed the murder of his father, gunned down in a 1923 robbery at a little grocery store he ran on East Jefferson near Maxwell Street. The murder shattered Ross's family. Ross was boarded out to relatives and his siblings were sent to the Marks Nathan Home. Ross ran errands for Al Capone, then became an amateur and professional boxer, a Golden Gloves champion, then champion of the world in three weight divisions, lightweight, light welterweight, and welterweight.

Ron Grossman, the *Tribune* historian and columnist, wrote: "In 1992, covering a reunion of Marks Nathan residents for the *Tribune*, I got to sit next to Ross's kid brother George. I was on a high for weeks afterward. George told me:

'On his way up, before every fight Barney would come to the orphanage. He was like a god to the kids at Marks Nathan.'"

Ross was billed as "the Pride of the Ghetto."

In 1942, Ross enlisted in the Marine Corps and fought with heroism at Guadalcanal, awarded a Silver Star by FDR in a Rose Garden ceremony. Ross was also childhood friends with Jack Ruby, born Jacob Rubenstein. Ruby was another neighborhood tough who grew up on Maxwell Street in a foster home, a juvenile delinquent arrested for truancy, a racetrack tout. Ross remained loyal to Ruby to the end, testifying as a character witness on his behalf at his trial for the killing of Lee Harvey Oswald.

At home that afternoon on Apple Tree Lane, watching a burly gunman in a dark fedora step forward and shoot Oswald in the belly, my father leapt to his feet from the sofa: "My god, that's Jack Ruby!" My father always "knew somebody who knew somebody who could fix something," someone from the days of Marks Nathan, someone with "hot" diamonds or emeralds to unload, which Dad would excitedly bring home, gifts for my mother, which thrilled her. These Chicago hoods had links to Mickey Cohen, Bugsy Siegel, and Meyer Lansky, associations that tantalized me, real mobsters and their dazzling women. Lansky, the Hyman Roth character portrayed by Lee Strasberg in *The Godfather Part II,* was born in Grodno, the beleaguered shtetl just up the road from Knyszyn. His birth name was Meier Suchowlanski. We were practically related. Dad somehow knew the assassin of Lee Harvey Oswald but slunk back into the sofa, back into his hardened shell, without another word about it, ever.

My father's circle of acquaintance at Marks Nathan included the photographer Mickey Pallas. They met, Dad told me, as five-year-olds in the bed-wetters' dorm, a shared ignominy. Mickey Pallas was the Weegee of Chicago and the founder of Gamma, the city's largest photo processing lab with over 125 employees. "His interest in photography," reads Pallas's 1997 *Tribune* obituary, "began when he was living at the Marks Nathan Jewish Orphan Home in Chicago. He and a buddy chipped in together and purchased a camera for $1.26."

Mickey photographed all Chicago: every celebrity and politician who came through town, blacks being baptized on the South Side, a family of white suburbanites posing in the driveway of their new ranch house, sitting in a Buick convertible. Studs Terkel wrote: "Ever on the go, Mickey, with the gait and build of a fighter, was deceptively good. So good that he captured, indelibly, a piece of history. Mickey Pallas, like Kilroy, was there."

On a trip to San Francisco in 2016, I made plans to meet Rusty Pallas, Mickey's son. Over a bowl of pho in a Vietnamese restaurant in the Sunset, Rusty told me that the Marks Nathan Home was no huge deal in his family, that his father didn't talk about it much at all, and that it had little to no impact on him or his father. Rusty went on to tell me, however, that he has an adopted son, and that "maybe I got the idea to adopt from my father's childhood in the orphanage." Along with my cousins, and Susan Baron, Rusty was the only child of a Home Kid I would meet, and all of us were impacted by the Home one way or another. Some Home Kids tried to ignore or surmount those years, to act as if they never happened, but my father would not. He ended every argument by declaring: "I am an orphan. Don't hold it against me!"

Some pretended the Home left them unfazed, they were tougher than that, but truth-tellers, like Dad, knew that was not the case.

The recorded history of the Marks Nathan Home amounts to a few faded clippings. All the firsthand witnesses are gone, the written shreds lost, recycled, or amiss in someone's basement. All that's left are my imperfect memories passed down to me by my troubled father, and the few dim memories retained by other children of the Home Kids, like the diminished recollections of my cousins, who may remember less than me. What was it like to live in the Home? I'm not exactly certain. What is it like to be the child of a Home Kid? Not always great, I can tell you.

The alumni reunions organized by Favil David Berns were emotional, upbeat affairs where ex–Home Kids vied with each other to grab the microphone to extol the Home and tell the audience how it saved their lives. Berns always invited reporters from the *Tribune* or the *Sun-Times* to record the event. It always made great copy, tearjerker stuff.

"Orphans Gather for Family Reunion" read the headline that accompanied Ron Grossman's 1992 piece.

"From 1906 till after World War II," Grossman wrote, "the orphanage on Chicago's West Side was a refuge for Jewish children whom life had handed a lousy deal."

In November 1978, an invitation arrived at our house on Apple Tree Lane for a reunion at the Highland Park Country Club.

"So c'mon you Swerdlows, Schmidts, Siegels and Friedmans," it read, "let's make it a good seder dinner."

Despite the fact that Dad was a member of the Highland Park Country Club and that the club was only ten minutes from our house, he absolutely refused to attend. I wish he had. I wish he had taken me with him.

———

Aaron Gruenberg was another Marks Nathan Home Kid and lifelong friend of Favil David Berns. With Berns's encouragement, Gruenberg, in 1982, began organizing the *Marks Nathan Oral History Project*, the same year I wrote Berns with tough questions about my father's experience in the Home and received the reply from Berns that copied his friend Aaron Gruenberg.

My private view is that Berns was disturbed and motivated by my 1982 letter questioning the quality of my father's Marks Nathan years, and that he and Gruenberg then decided to document the history of the Home as best they could, warts and all, hence Gruenberg's *Oral History Project*. After years of revisionist history and proud alumni boosterism, Gruenberg and Berns may finally have wanted to get the Home's history completely straight, for their fellow Home Kids, for themselves, and for their children like me.

The only known copy of this manuscript is on deposit in the archives of Jewish Child & Family Services in its downtown

Chicago office, made available to me by researcher Barbara Chandler. The *Oral History Project* strikes a far more somber tone than the backslapping, congratulatory, rags-to-riches story line of the festive alumni dinners hosted by Berns and reported by *Tribune* columnist Grossman. Gruenberg conducted interviews with nineteen alumni, including Dad's friend Mickey Pallas, and published their first-person accounts more or less verbatim. Collectively, they tell a sad, sometimes brutal, tale of emptiness and barely making do in the idiosyncratic, heavily inflected, Chicago-gangster speak of that epoch. This single volume recreates the dark history of the Home better than any individual perspective. Gruenberg wrote in his introduction:

> When members of the group left the Home, they left with both similar and dissimilar sets of experiences as well as different perceptions of them. Memories of the Home Kids are far from uniform. It is not surprising that some alumni remain bitter or cynical from the misfortune of their early lives. Some were subjected to tremendous suffering. But the majority of Home Kids grew up to achieve a high level of personal, and often public, success and are justifiably proud of their lives.

Most Home Kids shared a similar story line: their fathers died in their thirties, their mothers were institutionalized with nervous breakdowns. Ten-year-olds were found wandering the streets of Chicago, picked up and hospitalized for diphtheria, then moved into the Home. Lack of money was a problem for all.

Gruenberg asked the contributors to the *Oral History Project* four questions:

1) How did you come to live at Marks Nathan?
2) What was it like growing up in Marks Nathan?
3) Who took care of you?
4) What did the Home do for you?

In his interview, the photographer Mickey Pallas told Gruenberg a more daunting story about his Home years than the one he told his son, Rusty: "I was kind of knocked around. I lived for a time with my mother on Roosevelt Road. When I was four or five she was institutionalized. She had a breakdown and at that time a breakdown meant, 'Hey, you're crazy, man,' and that's it, see?"

A few Home Kids spoke candidly about the sheer panic they experienced when entering the Home for the first time: "It was a very traumatic experience. I was then about seven or eight years old. For one reason or another they couldn't take care of me," Gil Drucker said.

"My life was in turmoil," Art Friedman related. "So eventually, unbeknownst to me, the decision was made to put me in the Home. It was in the morning and they called me over to the car and they said 'get in the car' and they took me to the Home, and that was my first introduction to the Marks Nathan Home."

"I remember vividly the day I came to the Home," Bernie Gordon reported. "I remember coming with my brother and wandering around, terrified of being left alone there."

David Rubin entered the Home at age eight: "The first thing I knew I was marched right into the Home. I was too young to realize what was happening. I didn't know how or why or when or anything. They made me change clothes, that's all I remember. I was wearing short pants. I was bewildered."

Elmer Gertz grew up to become the lawyer who defended Henry Miller in the *Tropic of Cancer* obscenity case. He told Gruenberg: "See, I remember vividly the day I came to the Home. This huge institution."

The kids were small and lost and vulnerable, unloved, often parentless, now institutionalized, where and for how long they did not know.

Discipline in the Home was maintained by adult supervisors, some kind and enlightened, but others brutal and violent.

Aaron Gruenberg wrote the following about his own experience: "Home Kids were kept in line by physical punishment and by the constant anticipation of it. Discipline left an indelible, bitter mark on some. Those who had suffered in their young lives prior to coming to Marks Nathan were particularly vulnerable."

"They didn't think twice about slapping a kid or banging him one," Eddie Doctor said.

"If he was tough and slammed heads he was considered a good supervisor," said Bernie Rattner.

Miriam Markowitz Grossman said: "This was my first introduction to a world filled with people who were in charge of little ones who did not know what they were doing. They made life miserable for little people."

They certainly made life miserable for little ones like my dad and aunt Minna, my uncles Irv and Si.

David Rubin told Gruenberg: "The Home hired a supervisor named Bedford. He came in during the War, 1917 or something like that. He came from an orphanage in New York and he was really a mean, sadistic type. He would actually line us up, the whole dormitory or the whole class of 150 kids, and we would face the wall standing up for an hour or so because somebody misbehaved. Bedford was the guy's name. He was very tough. He actually hit some of the girls in the Home."

Sixty years after leaving the Home, Hannah Rosenthal Posner still recalled one supervisor vividly: "Oh, Miss Mabel Morris, she was a mean one. There were twenty beds in the dormitory. Between each bed was a wooden chair, and she used to punish us by making us stand in front of the chair making sure that nobody would sit down. Sometime we would stand like that for the whole afternoon."

Sally Drew Ryce was in the Home with her little sister, who was frequently physically punished. "I hated how they treated my sister," she said. "I was a tough kid. I stood up to them. Finally, I walked into the Supervisor's office and told him: 'Do not hit my sister any more.' And they stopped."

"I was always being punished," Hannah Rosenthal Posner recalled. "So I remember Mr. Feinstein constantly saying in the dining room, 'You kids have it made. There's a Depression going on and you never have to worry about food; the food's always there; you always have something to eat and you'll go out of the Home and think the world owes you a living, but they don't owe you a damned thing just because you were in an orphan home.' This always stayed with me."

Many Home Kids recounted the humiliating treatment of the bed-wetters, in particular. Bernie Gordon said:

"They would force a kid who wet his bed to put his face down in the urine in the moist mattress and keep it there. I don't recall for how long but the kid had his face pushed in it, literally."

Ester Leimberg Versten recalled: "A lot of children had problems wetting their beds. I wasn't one of them but I knew two kids in that category, and the older one used to stutter because she was so nervous. Even as a child I thought it was cruel for them to do what they did. The children that wet their beds had to put the sheets up to dry over the tops of their beds so that everybody knew that those kids had wet their beds. The other kids would make fun of them. That was no way to treat them."

In summary, Gruenberg wrote: "Home Kids almost invariably responded that they regretted not having a complete natural family."

"The only thing I really feel I missed was affection," said Maxine Speigel Fineberg. "After I left the Home I looked for it from every boy I went out with. If he put his arm around me I felt like I owed him something. That was the really bad thing about an orphan home. They couldn't love you."

Gruenberg added: "Modern medical science and psychiatry now recognize children of broken homes as being emotionally ill."

A woman named Mildred Winograd said: "This is what I truly missed in life, the fact that I didn't have a mother when I really and truly needed her."

Gruenberg's *Oral History Project* validated my father's entire testimony and all his tears. My father was damaged, with reason, not nuts, as his unloving wife, my own mother, claimed. He needed special care and understanding, as I knew all along. Finding this single volume in a Jewish archive validated me, as well as him. I was right about my father. My defense of his hurt to David Favil Berns was correct. Maybe I played some small role in the production of the *Oral History Project,* and in this way came, as I always intended, to the rescue of the brilliant, loving man who was my father.

The Marks Nathan Home closed its doors in 1948. I was born three years later at the University of Chicago hospital. We lived in the Beverly neighborhood. Three years after that, we moved to Glencoe.

My father was accepted into the Home February 25, 1920, ten weeks after his fifth birthday. He was a skittish little kid with a huge head, like me, hat size 7 7/8, the both of us, although I grew into my hat size and Dad never did. His very first night at Marks Nathan may not have been the traumatic affair it was for other newly arrived orphans because his brothers and sister, Sol, Irving, Simon, and Minnie were already in residence, having all moved in November 21, 1918, marched in together like a shabby little army. I reckon they consoled their baby brother as best they could when he arrived and welcomed him with as much love and tenderness as they could muster that first night.

The orphanage file for the Friedman family shows that Jenny scrambled, in a panic, after her husband Sam's death. She registered with the Home as a widow with six children to support only months after his death in 1916, and attempted

Photo of the SS *Breslau*, the ship my grandfather Kasiel took steerage from Bremen to Baltimore in 1903.

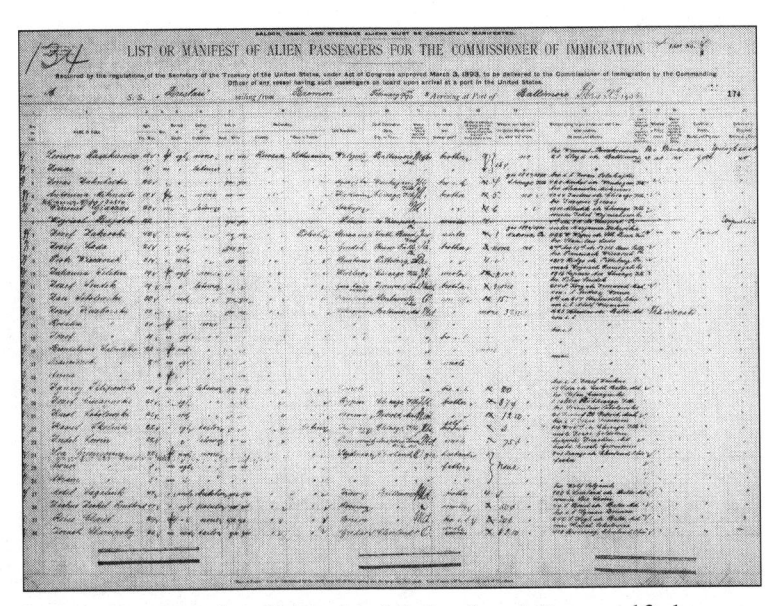

Passenger manifest from the SS *Breslau*. My grandfather Kasiel Skolnick is noted on line 22.

Studio portrait circa 1911 of Kasiel Skolnick (by now Sam Friedman) with wife, Jenny, and three children, Sol, Minna, and Annette.

My father's application form for admittance to the Marks Nathan Home, 1920.

Jenny and her orphans in Douglas Park outside the Home, 1920.

The four Friedman brothers in 1920; from top to bottom: Sol, Irving, Si, and Dan.

The Marks Nathan Home, circa 1920.

The Marks Nathan Home, circa 1920.

Sol, Cantor of Marks Nathan, circa 1921.

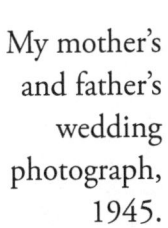

My mother's and father's wedding photograph, 1945.

IBM cards were the currency of my father's business at Associate Salvage Company (Credit: Max D Solomko / Shutterstock.com).

One constant in my father's mercurial life: a black Cadillac Coupe de Ville (Credit: Sergey Kohl / Shutterstock.com).

My mother in the box at Arlington Park, 1966.

My father in 1980.

My father visiting me in Charlottesville, 1984.

Samuel Friedman's new headstone in Waldheim Cemetery, taking the place of the blank slab that had marked his grave.

to get her two oldest kids, Sol and Minna, into the Home as early as April 1, 1917, but their application was rejected. On November 18, 1918, she was described in the Jewish Orphan's Research Bureau Report as "physically unable." Jenny signed my father's eight-page application for admittance in a florid, primitive script: "Friedman." The relief she must have felt when they finally took my little father off her hands.

"What means of support has the surviving parent?" the Marks Nathan application inquired.

"None" was my grandmother's reply.

"Has either parent a life insurance policy and to what amount?"

"None."

"Was the parent a member of any Order or Society?"

"No."

"If so, how much endowment or benefit will the surviving parent or child receive?"

"None."

"What other means were left the child? Specify amount."

"None."

"Has the child any relative able to support it?"

"No."

Jenny and my father had zero anything. Where could he have gone if not to the Marks Nathan Home?

Sam's cause of death was listed three times on the application, twice as pneumonia and once as pulmonary tuberculosis. Sam's death certificate lists pulmonary TB as the primary cause and emphysema as a secondary cause. Examining these two documents side by side, I felt relief: syphilis was off the table. And yet, I still could not shake the memory of Dad's whisper to me, he never lied, when I was old enough to understand, that his father, Sam Friedman, Kasiel Skolnick from Knyszyn, the shamed one, who lay for decades in an unmarked grave, died of syphilis, and that's why no one ever spoke his name.

Five-year-old Dad's application to the Home, executed by his mother, was full of revelation. At the time of his admittance, it turns out, the streets of Chicago were thick with our people, none of whom came to the assistance of the five Friedman orphans in Marks Nathan. Kasiel Skolnick, in fact, had two sisters, Mrs. Isaacson and a Mrs. Rosenthal, who were both alive and well. Jenny's parents, Moshe and Dinah Pinckovitch, my father's maternal grandparents, were living in the neighborhood in 1920. Jenny's three sisters and three brothers were also around—Mrs. Morris Patinkin; Mrs. Max Patinkin; Mrs. Isaacson; and Mike, Simon, and Jacob Pinckovitch—all lived nearby, within one mile of each other. All these close relatives, it was written on my father's intake form, did not "show great attachment" to my father or to any of his siblings.

This is the devastating answer and testimony under the category "Relatives (Type of service which they would be capable of rendering. Attitude towards Family. Fitness)."

"Do not show great attachment."

My father's grandparents, four aunts, and three uncles, all waived interest in Jenny's children for lack of attachment or affection, passing them over to the authorities at Marks Nathan. None ever visited the children in the Home, according to Dad. The Friedman orphan children, my father with his enormous drive and ambition, my great book- and chess-loving uncles, my charming little aunt Minna, and all that they would go on to create, me and Gregory and Mark and Richard and their kids and Nat and Peachie and Victoria, and Peachie's kids, were no different in 1920 than a cardboard box of abandoned kittens that someone was trying to unload on Lower Wacker Drive.

Jenny, in her defense, had no easy time of it. Described on her youngest son's orphanage intake form as "refined – rheumatism – cancer breast? – very much interested in children – great devotion," Jenny had four different addresses during my father's six Marks Nathan years, each apartment cheaper and of poorer quality than the one before, according to inspectors from the Home. She worked as a seamstress at George Lewis & Sons, manufacturer of silk undergarments, at 1300 West Jackson Boulevard. Jenny was paying twenty dollars a month in rent for her last apartment at 5918 South Justine. Complete financial responsibility for her children fell to the "State." She had a telephone number for the first two of those years, Humboldt-0999, which was then disconnected.

Other than his mother, my father assigned blame to no one for his abandonment in the Home, not his Pinckovitch grandparents, nor his Patinkin uncles or aunts. Dad profoundly understood the times and lessons of those days—you had to stand on your own and fight. No one would come to your rescue. There was no excess anything for you from anyone else's table. These cautions he made sure to pass down to me. It was I who was forever confounded by Dad's neglect as a child, not him. We will never know why Jenny was totally abandoned, left alone by her family to care for those six kids. Some things we will just never know.

After six years, my father was released from the Home into the custody of his oldest brother Sol, who got out himself at age seventeen, on August 7, 1923. Sol enrolled in night classes at John Marshall Law School and became financially self-sufficient by selling vacuum cleaners and dust mops door-to-door to West Side tenement dwellers for Commonwealth Edison. Sol was very successful at this endeavor because he would climb the stairs to the highest floors of the tenements where other salesmen never went. He lived in the Home four years, seven months, and fourteen days, passed the Bar Exam at nineteen, and grew up to become one of the most successful divorce attorneys in the city.

Jenny signed Dad's release documents, but Sol was the family breadwinner by then, and it was Sol's decision to get dad out of Marks Nathan first, thinking he was the most fragile of the siblings, and bring him under his wing. At eleven, my father still had some childhood left. Sol supported Dad and Jenny and gradually got his other siblings out, too, one by one. Si was the last to get out. By the time he did, in 1928, Si was irreparably damaged. My father knew Si's sacrifice to the rest of his family and loved him tenderly. My father thought Sol, his liberator, was a god. By the 1930 census, Sol was listed as head of the household on South Justine Street. It took years, but Sol finally reunited the entire family there.

The operation of this new household on South Justine Street in 1926, with Sol looking after his mother, and his little brother Dan just released from six years in the orphan home, is something I would give all my worldly goods to witness, if only for a minute.

"Dad," I asked, "why did you get out of the Home before Irving, Si, and Minna?"

"Because I cried the most."

The squeaky wheel gets the oil, as Dad always said.

Once Dad got out of the Home his life began in earnest, unencumbered. He wouldn't call it that, he wouldn't say he did, but he flourished. Dad was finally free. It did not take him long. By the time he graduated from high school, he was motivated, incentivized, and had direction in life.

In April 1945, just after their marriage, my father and mother moved in with Sol and his wife Catherine in order to save money before buying their first house. They may have stayed with Sol and Catherine for a year or longer. My father, the most independent man I've ever known, never requested assistance of anyone in his lifetime other than Sol.

In the early morning of May 16, 1962, I was awakened by my father wailing from his bedroom as if he'd been dealt an enormous blow and was dying. It was not quite 5:00 a.m. This is what a heart attack sounds like, I thought. He had just gotten a call from someone in Chicago. His oldest brother Sol was dead. My mother was standing over my father's bed in the complete darkness trying to console the inconsolable. It was late spring on the calendar, but it was still winter in Chicago.

"Does this mean I get to stay home from school?" I asked him hopefully, age eleven.

"Go on, get out of here," Dad said from his bed, disgusted with me.

I only wanted to see his face, but in the darkness I couldn't. I wanted to watch him handle this loss. What did Sol's death mean? It was like the death of a pharaoh or a king.

I got dressed and walked around the corner to West School, getting there just as the sun was coming up, never arriving at school so unnaturally early, the playgrounds and teacher's parking lot empty. I got to school an hour or so before the janitors arrived. Somehow the time passed, me on the swing set, the playground frozen stiff. I thought of my father alone in his grief as if back in the Home, my uncle Sol, whom I barely knew, and my older cousin Greg, then only fifteen years old, whom my mother and father loved so much. Greg was adored by them because he was the second coming of Sol. They recognized Sol in him. He embodied Sol's bristling intelligence and energy. Greg was the torchbearer for the next generation of Friedman men. We would all go on to live the stories of our lives, but Greg was Sol's son, first son of the first son, and many years later, he would show me, his cousin, the same love and devotion that his father showed mine. Sol saved Dad's life by pulling him from the Marks Nathan Home when my father was eleven years old. Decades later, Greg would arrive and validate me, by coming to my second marriage and telling the assembled wedding party the dramatic story of our fathers' heroic lives, about their years in the Marks Nathan Home, and about their profound love and care for one another.

Five

Arlington Park

When I was fourteen years old, Dad bought a box at Arlington Park, the thoroughbred racetrack outside Chicago, where we went every Saturday and spent the entire day together, him and me. A couple of times I cut school and hung out there by myself, but it wasn't as much fun without Dad. Many friends would tell me years later that they remembered this crazy chapter of my life as a racetrack tout and thought it was an odd form of entertainment for a father and son. I admit, I was far luckier than most kids to have such a father who would throw me into the deep end at Arlington Park among its characters and criminals. At Arlington, I got to wander around and experience an adult world without supervision. My father taught me everything there was to know about the city of Chicago by taking me everywhere with him and turning me loose. He learned firsthand Chicago didn't kill him. I would learn firsthand, too.

We'd arrive at the track in time for lunch at the Post and Paddock Club, the most elegant dining room in the world, as far as I was concerned at age fourteen, with the world's greatest view, where I always had the roast beef, also best in the world, with mashed potatoes and gravy, and we'd leave late in the afternoon after the featured race, the eighth, and drive back to Glencoe, listening to the car radio, exhausted. Our racing weekend would really start Friday night, when Dad and I would drive up to the big newsstand on Main Street in Evanston and buy a fresh copy of Saturday's *Racing Form,* and maybe a copy of the *Green Sheet,* a tip sheet, almost always wrong. We'd take the *Form* home and study the shit out of it from beginning to end, me making notes in the margins, drawing diagrams, thinking it an exact science, preparing my betting plan for the next day, talking the whole thing over carefully with Dad afterwards, he in his bedroom in his black Eames lounger, WFMT on in the background, sharing with him what I had learned. Dad was much more casual about the *Form* than I. He didn't really study it; he didn't give it proper consideration, I thought. He would have been a more successful bettor, in my opinion, if he examined the *Form* with greater care. All the mysteries of the races about to unfold before our eyes were encrypted in the past performance of every horse noted in the *Form's* special hieroglyphics. Deciphering this precise code took hours. Unraveling it made me feel like a genius. I suppose Dad left the *Form* to me as part of our inchoate collaboration.

I loved the track. I loved the pageantry. I loved the beautifully groomed horses in their colors, the people who inhabited the track, the trainers in their tweed flat caps and the gaunt jockeys and the railbirds and big shot owners smoking cigars, and I loved being among the huge crowd at Arlington Park. I also loved Arlington's track announcer, Phil Georgeff, whose voice was electrifying.

"And here they come!" Georgeff would call, "spinning out of the turn and into the stretch!"

What words! What a moment in sports as in life! Everyone had hope, no horse was yet out of the running, but within a few strides, the jockey's whips now lashing at their haunches, hands urging them on, releasing the steeds within seconds of Georgeff's cry, half the field badly faded, often dragging your favorite with them to the back of the pack, with no hope of win, place, or show, but many lengths out of the money, your ticket worthless in your sweaty palm.

"That's life," is the way I figured it.

On to the next race.

Dad's box at Arlington had seven or eight seats. The two other regulars were bald Jackie Lacko and short, heavyset Al Fox. Jackie was Dad's foreman at Associated Salvage down by the Union Stock Yards, "cousin Jack," I called him, as he was a distant relation of my mother, and Foxie was a sketchy old pal of Dad's from somewhere on the West Side, who drove himself to the track every Saturday in a filthy, block-long, weather-beaten, gold Cadillac sedan. Al was a little guy who drank quietly, bet heavily, and lost a lot of money every week. Watching Al get wiped out every Saturday and go home silent, broke, and miserable, losing five hundred dollars on a summer afternoon when five hundred dollars was a lot of money, taught me that gambling was a fool's game.

Cousin Jack completely fixated on a horse called Oink, a big chestnut in the downward trajectory of a long racing career, one-time winner of the United Nations Handicap, still a gamer at seven or eight, who would run in one of the stakes races every Saturday. Jackie would go wild when Oink was in contention. "Here they come! Spinning out of the turn into the stretch!" Georgeff would cry over the loudspeaker before a crowd of fifteen thousand, and Jackie's cry would equal his, standing high on his orange plastic seat in the box, slapping his hand with his rolled up *Green Sheet* whipping Oink home: "Come on, Oink! Come on, you *momzer!*" he'd shout. Oink was almost always in the money, and Jackie was always exhilarated. Watching Jackie whip Oink home was a highlight of our day.

Mom came to the track with us once a year at most, only after my pleading with her. She generally stayed home with my brother, who was too small to wander around Arlington Park. But others would come. My scholarly uncle Irving would bring my cousins Mark and Richard, where the three of us, age fourteen, never discussed the ramifications of our mixed religious heritage, the terribly complicated fact that our fathers married outside the faith. That conversation would wait until we were sixty; for now we picked out a few horses and made a few bets. We were innocents together. They were a bit jealous of me now that my dad was the grandee with the box on the finish line at Arlington, but I was always glad they were around, I loved them so. I loved showing them my new expertise around the park, demonstrating which betting window would take a two dollar bet from a fourteen-year-old kid, how easy it was to buy a beer, how to hang out in the bar smoking Parliaments and drinking beer without looking completely stupid. They were suitably impressed with all the new Chicago secrets I had gleaned.

Late at night, just after the sleeping pills kicked in but hadn't yet completely knocked him out, dad would handwrite long, rambling letters to Chicago Jewish intellectuals he admired, describing the agony of his childhood in the Marks Nathan Home, his life story since leaving the Home, and asking a few polite questions of these learned men. He wrote these letters, I think, with a genuine desire to obtain expert counsel about his puzzling life, the exact material, in other words, that I asked him about which he never discussed with me. The meds certainly had a loosening effect on his pen and ability to express himself. He went downstairs to the spare bedroom after my mother had gone to sleep and wrote and mailed these letters without telling anyone until long afterward. Dad also may have thought himself engaging in the high-minded dialogue he deserved with the greatest thinkers and innovators of our time, taking his place at the High Table among them.

Two of these men, University of Chicago economist Milton Friedman and Chicago author Saul Bellow, were nice enough to write back. Dad was shocked to receive return letters in our mailbox on Apple Tree Lane from Friedman and Bellow in the same week. Dad probably forgot he had written to them in the stupor of his secobarbital haze. In his letter to Milton Friedman, Dad asked for stock market investment advice. Friedman demurred in the nicest of ways, saying he was not much good at predicting short-term market movements. In his letter to Bellow, Dad invited him to Arlington Park, and Bellow accepted. Dad was shocked.

What in the world was he going to say to Saul Bellow? he asked me with alarm, holding Bellow's letter in his hand. Bellow was coming next Saturday.

Bellow's novels, of course, are filled with Chicago characters not unlike Dad, and Bellow relished Chicago city life in all its grim majesty. Dad and Bellow had a couple of things in common: they were the same age, and they both attended Crane College for one semester in 1932 in the depths of the Depression before the college went bankrupt at the end of the year. At that point, their lives diverged, to put it mildly. Bellow continued his education at the University of Wisconsin while my father went into the junk business. Dad began working for his uncle Max Patinkin, grandfather of the great Mandy, and was eventually inspired to go into business for himself by another famous Jewish writer, Arthur Miller, after seeing *Death of a Salesman* on stage in Chicago with my mother. My father became a business success using Willy Loman as an example of what he did not want to become. He never went back to college. Graduation from Lindblom High School, class of 1932, followed by one semester at Crane College, was as far as my father's formal education extended.

Bellow wasn't intimidating when he slipped into the box with us that afternoon at Arlington Park, his celebrity undetected by the vast racing crowd, but he was so august no one knew what to say to him. He wasn't slumming with us. He was polite and interested to meet Dad and hear his stories about the Home years. "I knew the Marks Nathan Home," he told Dad, giving him an overture, but Dad hadn't organized his thoughts in advance, so the conversation stalled and went nowhere.

Bellow smiled at me in a natural way from under his black fedora and was dressed far better than any man I had ever seen in Glencoe. Normally ebullient Jackie Lacko, always shouting his guts out as the horses hit the turn, fell silent as a choirboy when Bellow arrived. Al Fox was practically invisible. We never really got it going. The laureate of Chicago hung around long enough for two or three races, then everyone solemnly stood and shook hands. He was courteous to Dad and us. I've read all of Bellow's books with an eye for Dad or a detail from that day. Meeting Bellow like that always made me feel connected to him and proud. He was Dad's Nobel Prize–winner, and I knew he deserved it because of his complete authenticity, his willingness to meet someone like Dad who sought him out, and his interest in all men, the high, the low, and everyone in between, an open, egalitarian mindset shared by Chicago's finest homegrown intellectuals, the attitude that typified the Chicago school.

Later that summer I became obsessed with a horse, a tiny, big-hearted turf specialist named Fusilier Boy, a grandson of Princequillo, one of the greatest studs in the history of thoroughbred breeding, and first cousin to the yet unborn Secretariat. This little horse was my chief discovery that summer of 1966. Fusilier Boy had performed gamely every Saturday, coming from the back of the pack, a thrilling stretch-runner overtaking horses but coming up short, just running out of ground, every outing. No one but me seemed to notice what was happening. If I had run a hedge fund instead of being a fourteen-year-old placing illegal bets at Arlington Park, I'd have been a billionaire.

Fusilier Boy was surrounded by good karma. He was owned by the colorful Louisiana politician Harvey Peltier and was trained by Johnny Meaux, a noted figure around Arlington, dubbed the "canny Cajun" by the *Tribune*'s racing columnist. This beautiful horse was small but had Princequillo's massive heart, the heart that in his cousin Secretariat weighed twenty-two pounds, the autopsy showed, three times the weight of a normal thoroughbred's heart.

"Today's card," the *Tribune* turf writer elegantly reported, "offers the enigma named Fusilier Boy, the pony-sized grass runner who earned $128,230 last season but so far this year has been unable to find the winner's circle in a dozen starts."

Out of the money all summer but closing races like a rocket, Fusilier Boy went off at twenty-two to one in the $100,000 Lindheimer Cup that day, July 15, a sixteenth of a mile longer than any race of the season for him, just enough extra distance to accommodate Fusilier Boy's closing charge. I had done the math. I had studied the *Form*. I had seen the horse go. The distance was perfect for him.

Minutes before post time, wandering around the smoky innards of Arlington Park by myself, I saw little Johnny Meaux in a wrinkled suit drinking whiskey at the bar with a tall and gorgeous blonde dressed like she was going to a nightclub.

"Johnny!" I called, walking over to him and tugging at his tan jacket, shorter than him by a foot. "Is Fusilier Boy going to win?"

"Kid," he said, looking down at me like he'd known me my entire life, "bet everything you've got on him. He's going to win!" Johnny Meaux was certain of the outcome and would not lie to a boy like me.

Weaving my way through the crowd, I could not get back to the box fast enough. Dad was huddled in deep conversation with Jackie and Foxie.

"Dad, I just saw Johnny Meaux downstairs." I didn't say I saw him in the bar, and I omitted the blonde. "He says Fusilier Boy is going to win! We have to get downstairs right away and bet on him."

No one else in the box heard me. Jackie and Foxie already had their bets in. Big bets on bum horses that would lose badly that day. Dad, bless him, listened to me. He allowed me to pull him out of his plastic orange chair. We got our bets in, the largest bets I'd ever seen him make, just before closing.

Fusilier Boy had a flair for the dramatic. That's what I loved about him. The little guy came from out of nowhere on the far outside over that final sixteenth of a mile to overcome the entire field and win by a nose at long odds in a photo finish. Harvey Peltier made $100,000 that afternoon on a small horse purchased for him just a few months earlier by smart Johnny Meaux for $25,000. "The story of the year," the *Tribune* writer called it. I watched crumpled little Johnny Meaux, leaning on the blonde, stagger into the winner's circle for the photograph, knowing he could barely stand up.

My jubilation in the box was offset by the complete misery of Jackie and Foxie. Dad told me to quiet down, that I was the only person celebrating Fusilier Boy in the entire grandstand at Arlington Park. Jackie and Foxie bet the house on Oink, who ran fourth or fifth. My euphoria was further offset when we got in the car and turned on the radio. A mass murderer named Richard Speck had just raped and murdered eight student nurses somewhere on the vast South Side of Chicago. Dad stopped the car so I could step outside, my pockets filled with rolled-up twenties, and vomit.

Six

Apple Tree Lane

All I knew growing up was Glencoe, its public schools, its village library, its tidy downtown, the two delis, the ice cream shop, Ray's sporting goods, Wally King's records, Wieneke's hardware, the office of my pediatricians Dr. Harris and Dr. Rosenbloom, the movie theater, the golf club, and the beach. This was my universe, and whatever came after wasn't better than this. Wherever I arrived was no improvement upon Glencoe in any measurable, material way. My father set the bar very high by delivering us to Glencoe. If I can blame my father for anything, it is that he made it so difficult to surpass him. My children were afforded experiences my father could not have dreamed possible, but they did not exceed the happiness and life experiences my father provided me.

Glencoe was Dad's bedroom. He participated in no municipal event save the rare parent-teacher conference or Fourth of July parade, watching me march as a Cub Scout, holding the American flag. He'd leave the house by 4:30

a.m., sometimes much earlier, and arrive home no later than 3:30 p.m., exhausted. Beating the traffic in both directions was his life's purpose. Only idiots were stuck in traffic. Dad beat the hell out of his Cadillacs, replaced every year with a new one, never washed, their ashtrays stuffed with butts. In this neighborhood of Jewish breadwinners, all veterans of World War II, everyone drove a big American car until one day Mr. Wolfson down the street brought home a small red Mercedes-Benz convertible. Dad's eyes got wide. Suddenly, it was OK to buy a German car. Within a year, there were twenty Benzes on the street. He began buying Mercedes for my mother, first an eggshell blue 250C, a gem, which was deemed inadequate, then a red 450SL. These Mercedes were big steps up from her Chevys and required a colorful new wardrobe for her by Emilio Pucci, an Italian designer favored by Marilyn Monroe. Mom in her Mercedes going grocery shopping in Glencoe dressed in Pucci now looked like an air hostess for Braniff International Airways. Dad was making a jillion dollars then, and he spent it on us. He knew how to make money and was certain more was coming. Watching his comfort with money, doing his tabulations nightly in his emphatic, indecipherable scrawl on the back of an envelope in his Eames lounger, leaning over his shoulder, observing, made me comfortable with it, too. My beloved father was at his best then, a Chicago aristocrat, lowborn and obscure, a marvel to behold. For the first time, he was paying attention to his attire. Instead of flashy stuff from the old West Side haberdashers, his clothing now came from Brooks Brothers. With his horn-rimmed glasses, Dad started to look like he had gone to prep school or Yale.

He became superior and more unattainable with financial success and communicating with him required additional thought and effort. It was tougher than ever to get his attention. When I wanted or needed something only he could provide, I learned to slow down and listen, to treat him almost delicately, and to choose my words with caution. When I did all this, he'd turn his giant focus on me, and take me in, in an instant. My dad was a veteran of the Marks Nathan Home. He had survived the pits of despair. I was his beloved and indulged namesake firstborn son. He was there to protect my ass, unlike his father, the negligent Kasiel Skolnick, the no-show, who did not. Dad claimed he did not know how to be a father, but as I knew, he was the world's best, precisely because of his deprivation, overcompensating because he did not have a father of his own. He was learning on the job and never said no to me, not when it mattered. When I asked him something he always said yes.

Not long after getting my driver's license, Dad allowed me to take him into the Porsche dealer down the street from New Trier High School and show him the Porsche 914, unspeakably beautiful. This was Porsche's new entry-level car, and it cost a year's tuition at the University of Chicago, about $3,500. I told Dad that, however preposterous and objectionable any reasonable person might find it, I would love to have this car, it would be my dream come true, that I could not steal it and get away with it, that having such an accessory would greatly enhance my chances of success, for instance, with the vast and highly intriguing female population at New Trier, glorious beyond my ability to describe them. Dad heard me out, understood my deranged logic, a teenage boy once himself, and summoned the salesman. He bought the car on the spot giving it to me to drive home, my first experience with a manual transmission. I killed the engine repeatedly, in a sweat, until I got the feel of the sensitive clutch, barely getting the new Porsche out of the dealer parking lot onto Green Bay Road. The kid next door, in Hy Spector's old house, now that Hy and Mindy had moved into larger digs courtesy of the Lava Lite, had a new, silver Pontiac GTO, and my pal down the block, whose aged grandparents spoke Yiddish but no English, had a blue Corvette. But I in my green 914 raised the ante considerably. "Affluenza" was not then a word in anyone's vocabulary, and it did not apply to us anyway. We had been poor and we had been rich and we knew rich was better. When we first moved to Apple Tree Lane in 1958, everyone was striving, but no one was rich. In five or six years, all that changed.

It wasn't always that easy for me. Chicago was a tough town. My life as the son of an orphan meant that when I turned thirteen or fourteen, it was imperative to find after-school or weekend work that paid an hourly wage, no "internships," and a full-time job during the summer, no questions asked. All the kids on Apple Tree Lane, the children or grandchildren of the once impoverished, had real jobs, scooping ice cream, delivering papers, whatever. No occupation was too menial, nothing was beneath us. Some kids found jobs they liked, but not me.

My first job was at a busy Woolworths in a nearby shopping center where the manager gave me a paint scraper and told me to scrape off all the accumulated chewing gum that had been ground into the store's linoleum floors over the years, thousands of square feet of it, as far as the eye could see. My mother, who praised me to the heavens for obtaining this very first job, and who drove me to my first day of work like I was her hero, picked me up at the end of the day, horrified by the assignment given me by the store manager. After the entire day, I was only able to scrape the hardened chewing gum off a space about three feet square. It would take a kid like me years to clean the entire floor at Woolworths with a paint scraper. My mother took me home telling me that was my last day at Woolworths. I loved her for it.

That winter, courtesy of my cousin Bernie, I got a job checking coats at the International Amphitheater for the big Chicago Auto Show, back in the days before construction of McCormick Place. Bernie and I were assigned to the busy coat check desk at the front entrance with no training and no supervision. We were just turned loose to figure out the coat-checking process on the fly.

Since this was Chicago, and since the show took place in February, people came in wearing heavy parkas, scarves, hats, gloves, and rubber boots which they casually tossed at us behind the desk, hundreds of individual items, all mismatched within minutes, starting to pile up haphazardly on the floor. From the outset, in a panic, we completely screwed up the sequence of claim tickets, and before I knew it, my little cousin Bernie threw in the towel and walked off the job without saying a word, leaving me alone in the pile of winter apparel. For a minute or two I tried to sort out the mess, but when it dawned on me I couldn't, and that Bernie wasn't coming back, I abandoned my post, too. But instead of fleeing the International Amphitheater in shame and finding some way back to the North Shore alone, I looked around for Bernie and found him eating a hot dog at the far end of the arena as if nothing had happened. We casually appraised the new cars together, then, cautiously, moved a healthy distance from the coat check area to watch the mayhem as people drifted back to retrieve their belongings and go home. It was a total disaster, guys fighting over boots and coats, people leaving with the wrong hats and gloves after failing to find their own. After that, I always respected the intricacies of a well-run coat check operation.

The following summer I worked at the Glencoe Animal Hospital on Skokie Boulevard cleaning dog runs. I thought I'd try this because I liked dogs and because the animal hospital was near our home. I rode my bike there in the early morning before the place opened, let myself in, then went into the back where all the dogs howled at me from their cages, demanding attention. They desperately needed to be let out. I'd let them out, one by one, into individual outdoor runs where they would immediately shit. Finally, all fifteen or twenty dogs were moved outside. Next, I cleaned their now vacated indoor crates, many fouled overnight. After that, I'd move them all back inside again one by one. By this point, all the outdoor runs were filthy and need to be washed down with a high-powered hose. The entire process of moving the dogs outside then back in again, and cleaning all the indoor kennels and outdoor runs took a couple of hours. This was the type of job available to thirteen-year-old kids. I became extremely comfortable handling large, aggressive dogs, gently restraining animals that required inoculation, although cats were difficult to restrain, and cleaning large quantities of dog shit at any time of day. I don't recall what I was paid, but it wasn't enough.

One summer, I rode my bicycle to the Glencoe Golf Club and shagged practice balls for fifty cents a bag. Then I tried caddying. My first golfer client, clearly a moron, asked me, a tiny kid, to caddie double—to carry two large bags. I could not even carry one. I was dismissed by the time we reached the first green.

From these experiences I learned that all jobs were bad, that there was no such thing as a good job, that self-employment was the holy grail, the only way to live was by my wits, as Dad had done, from a far worse starting point than me. I learned this lesson from an early age. With a dad like mine, I didn't have to get an MBA or attend classes in entrepreneurship. As his son, I had watched entrepreneurship in action.

Just as Dad never wanted to talk about the Home or his childhood, he rarely wanted to take me to his place of business, the picturesque Associated Salvage Company on South Union Avenue at 41st Street, the entire neighborhood bathed in the grotesque aroma of the Union Stock Yards, diminished in the 1960s, but still in operation. When I got out of the car the first time that famous stench smashed me in the face.

"What the heck, Dad?"

But Dad did not even notice it. What kind of life had Dad led that would make him immune to the vile reek of the Union Stock Yards?

Dad would not take me to Associated Salvage because it was dirty; it was in a terrible part of town; he wasn't proud of it; he did not want me to see the place. Of course, I insisted we go, so once in a while he'd take me. We'd park in front of his building or across the street next to the litter-strewn Taylor-Lauridsen Park, scene of incalculable murders and muggings, but before getting out of the locked car, Dad would remove the black snub-nosed .32 caliber revolver he kept in the glove compartment and take it with him into the building, where I'd follow him up the filthy staircase to his office, two oak desks, two broken desk chairs, and two black telephones, where he stuck the weapon in his desk drawer. Dad called the place Associated because he wanted it to be the first name people saw when they looked for salvage companies in the yellow pages.

"Why do you have that thing, Dad?" I asked on my first visit, referring to the gun.

"You never know what could happen around here. It's just a precaution," he said.

I looked around the office, struck by how filthy the place was. You could not see out the windows, they were so grimy. It was obvious no one ever cleaned. I could not understand why Dad voluntarily would work in such a hellhole. But immediately I also liked the place. Dad's office smelled like his bedroom at home.

"Have you ever fired it?"

"Once. Into a stack of phone books in the back of the shop."

Dad had thirty black men, all from the Deep South, working in the plant baling paper. More than once, according to him, somebody went crazy, that's why he had the gun. Jackie Lacko was back there too, fearless shop foreman, superintending "the men." Jackie was important to Dad. He kept the operation running smoothly, the men in line, and the equipment in repair. Without him, Dad would have had no life outside the shop, no early retreats back to his quiet bedroom in Glencoe, no afternoon golf in Highland Park. This place, Associated Salvage, how it looked and ran and stank, was my real father. He invented this insane machine in a South Side slum that printed money. It was the product of his need and genius, symbol of his great resilience and complete mastery of the facts of life. The fact that he could make so much from so little amazed me. Of course he hated it, of course he didn't want to be there, of course he could brag about it to no one, of course he never wanted to introduce me to the place.

Associated consisted of three inground hydraulic waste paper presses that could compress eight thousand pounds of used paper into neat seven-foot-tall bales, a scale to weigh the bales, a three-bay loading dock, three miserable trucks that were never washed, and a few thousand feet of rodent-infested windowless storage space. That was it. The presses made a deafening whine when in action, but still above the din you could hear Jackie shouting instructions and warnings to the men. It took three men to operate each press, four men to move the bales onto dollies, two or three men to load the bales onto the trucks, and each truck had a driver and a helper, sometimes two. When the men gingerly tipped over one of the massive bales onto a dolly they'd brace themselves for its heavy fall and they'd shout "hey" or "ho" when they caught it, a dangerous maneuver. They moved a half-million pounds of loose, unsorted paper in, and thousands of neat bales out of the place, every week. Most of the paper arrived in the form of millions of cream-colored, punched IBM cards, the gold standard of waste paper, valued for its high quality, purchased for pennies a ton from any data center in Chicago, large or small, that operated an IBM computer.

The entities selling Dad these cards saw no value in them at all. They were trash clogging their hallways and warehouses. They wanted them out of the way. This was the magic formula and linchpin to Dad's business life. Dad collected and baled the cards and sold them to paper manufacturers who coveted them in Indiana, Wisconsin, and elsewhere in the city. There were many junk and scrap metal dealers in town, but no one else in Chicago was doing this with so-called scrap paper, and no one in Chicago was moving such volume. Dad was a revolutionary personality, one of the original recyclers. Dad was my first introduction to a "green" person, although that wasn't the way he saw himself.

Colored paper was less desirable than white or off-white paper. Thick paper was more valuable than thin paper. Cardboard—or corrugated cardboard—was virtually without value, but they'd bale it up just the same and sell it to somebody. Only newsprint was complete trash.

Dad told me that Associated Salvage was one of the most terrible places on earth, but I saw only its redeeming features. The South Side never scared me, the black men in the plant were unlike any men I had ever met before, the shop floor was the scene of constant activity, physical bravery, and manly industry from 6:00 a.m. until complete exhaustion. If this place, his invention, the product of his genius, his solution to his impoverishment, defined my father, then I admired him more than ever. Associated

Salvage was real life, none more real or raw. It was my father's life, and it was mine.

Out of work, in between completely crap summer jobs, I suggested to my father that I work for him until school resumed in September. I wanted to spend more time with my dad, I wanted to drive to work with him in the car, and I wanted to watch him operate the enterprise at Associated. I did not know this quite so explicitly at the time, but this was what I wanted to do. I was sixteen. I was going to spend all week working for Dad, on Saturday we'd go to the track, and on Sunday we'd golf at Highland Park Country Club. No one else I knew had a relationship with their father like the one I had with mine. Many dads wanted nothing to do with their kids, and most of the boys I knew had little interest in their fathers. My father and I were not like that. My father was the most fascinating person I had ever met in my life, the smartest, the least predictable, the most loving.

The night before he died, my father called me at my home in Charlottesville, Virginia from Highland Park on the North Shore, where he and my mother were then living. The call was a little later in the evening than normal.

"Just wanted to call you, son," he said, "wanted to hear your voice, tell you I love you."

"Sure, Dad," I replied, "I love you too."

We had this conversation thousands of times, but something about his tone was a little off. He was wistful and sounded far away. I put down the phone not understanding what had just happened. He died in his sleep. The aneurysm in his chest, the size of a grapefruit, had burst. My mother found him in his bed around 9:00 a.m. I was already at work when she called me. I tried calling my wife but could not reach her, then left my office to wander around Charlottesville in a stupor. I had lived in Charlottesville fifteen years by then and knew every nook and cranny of the little town. But on this occasion, wandering around the courthouse and near the hospital, I got completely lost. I did not know where I was. I was thirty-six years old with two children of my own and one more on the way. I walked alone like that for hours, unthinking, unsure of my whereabouts. It had been many years since Dad and I had spent any meaningful time together, save for a brief holiday and the increasingly rare trip back to Chicago.

The summer I was sixteen, Dad was fifty-two years old. To my surprise, he agreed to my employment scheme. The tough guy wanted my company as much as I wanted his. I was to start work as the boss's son on Monday. Through Associated Salvage I would get to know my father as the real man he was, a true king of the city. During those weeks he showed me a Chicago I never knew existed, people I could not imagine, lives not just from Bellow, but from Nelson Algren, Upton Sinclair, Gwendolyn Brooks, Richard Wright, Carl Sandburg, Mike Royko, and Studs Terkel, the great poets of our tragic city.

Somehow, very kindly and tenderly, he got me out of bed in the dark at 5:00 a.m., chomping at the bit to get going, and we drove South on the dead empty Edens Expressway in the big fast Cadillac. In thirty minutes we were on South Jefferson Street, stopping for breakfast at an insanely busy place called Manny's Cafeteria. Manny's was filled by every character and Chicago oddball: guys getting off work, guys going to work, firemen, policemen, peddlers, newsmen, derelicts. After the fastest breakfast on record, we left for Associated.

Jackie Lacko now looked at me like an insect, not his good buddy at the racetrack. He was thinking: what am I going to do with this kid? Dad assigned me to Jackie and told me to stick with him like glue, not to touch anything in the shop, that dangers lurked everywhere, that I could lose a limb by accident. I could fall in a press, be crushed against the dock by a truck, fall under a bale.

The men started drifting in all dressed in rags, unbathed, soiled, in slow motion, one or two wearing worn out bedroom slippers, too poor to own shoes. Most were entirely quiet this early in the morning. By 6:15 a.m. the place was in high gear, the presses whining, the men shouting, new bales being loaded into trucks. They weren't talking but they were working, quickly filling the old presses with cream-colored IBM cards, and I was trying to help them.

Work on the shop floor sorting cards, heaving twenty pound boxes of paper around, was faster paced and more demanding than I thought, and I was breathless after only a few minutes of trying to keep up. It was early morning. How was I going to make it through the entire day? I was the boss's son. I was supposed to set an example, not sit down or leave the building. At sixteen, I was a kid. The guys loading the presses were men.

The men called Dad "Danny," sometimes with real affection, which surprised me. I thought Dad's interaction with the men would be adversarial given the history of race relations and segregation in Chicago, but I was wrong. They liked him and treated him with respect. Dad stayed in his office and off the floor most of the time. He was usually on the phone calling offices around Chicago trying to find new sources of processed cards and quality waste paper. After a successful call, he'd send over one of his trucks to make the pickup. Oftentimes loads were half what was described to him. Obviously, bigger loads were always better. When Dad came out on the floor to watch the action or talk to Jackie, one of the men would always have something to say to him. One sidled up to Dad and told him he was short of money, and asked for a little help. Dad immediately unpeeled a twenty-dollar bill from his roll and handed it over. Another, drunk, was sarcastic with Dad, maybe looking for a fight. It was interesting to watch my father at that moment, and I studied his response. He rose up and made himself large, turning away after staring him down. My little father was no fighter, but he could and would defend himself. I saw that now. He would not back down. He was always on guard on the floor, in the car, in life.

Dad saw I was not much use in the plant, so the next day he put me on a truck with his most trusted driver, Johnny Crenshaw, and a helper named Bobby. Most of Dad's men worked for him a few weeks then were gone forever, replaced by an endless stream of impoverished black men up from Mississippi and Georgia. But Johnny Crenshaw and E. B. Watson worked for Dad for thirty years. In the pecking order of things at Associated Salvage, there was Dad, Jackie Lacko, E. B. Watson, and Johnny Crenshaw, all respected and looked after by one another. Johnny and E. B. helped us move into Glencoe, the shabby truck from Associated Salvage making a delivery of our furniture to brand new Apple Tree Lane. That was a spectacle, the ruined truck spewing black fumes bouncing down the wide street into our spotless subdivision.

We were on our way to a new industrial park on the Northwest Side of Chicago, an hour's drive. I rode in the cab between Johnny and Bobby, nobody talking. Bobby was as alien a species to me as I undoubtedly was to him. I was hoping my presence wasn't putting a damper on the mood inside the big truck.

When we arrived at the XYZ Corporation headquarters, Johnny immediately found the big new loading dock at the rear, he honked, and the doors opened to a vast, clean storage facility. We were greeted by a white man in a white shirt and tie who wanted nothing to do with us but who pointed out the boxes of cards he wanted us to remove. There were thousands of them. Thousands of twenty-pound boxes of clean, white, punched IBM cards.

"Man," Johnny said. "This is a huge load. Might have to make another trip or two here. Your dad will like to see this!"

So Johnny backed the truck to the dock, and we got going.

We loaded the boxes onto dollies, about eight at a time, rolled the dollies onto the truck, and stacked the boxes on top of each other from floor to ceiling. Johnny stayed in the truck and did the stacking. Bobby and I wheeled the boxes to Johnny in the rear of the truck. Each box of cards was heavy for me. I could handle one box of cards at a time, barely. Bobby could handle three or four. Bobby was built like an NFL linebacker. I was a skinny teenager. When Bobby saw me emulating him and struggling to lift two boxes, he came immediately to my assistance by taking them off my hands, helping me heave them up to Johnny. Even so, I tired quickly, my arms trembling, turning into rubber bands. Bobby never stopped passing three boxes at a time high overhead to Johnny who stacked them ever so neatly in the truck. The truck had to be loaded with precision, Johnny told me. This was a heavy load, and the truck could flip if the load was uneven.

"Bobby, you are the strongest man I have ever seen!" I told him truthfully. He was twenty-two years old, Dad told me, from somewhere in Alabama. He was not only strong, but also big-hearted. He saw me struggling and helped without diminishing me or making me feel badly about not carrying my own weight. These were superlative traits in any human being, I thought. Bobby had opened my eyes. I looked at him with admiration. Maybe Chicago wasn't about to erupt in violence as Dad believed. Maybe black men and white men could work together and help each other.

We loaded the truck from front to rear, floor to ceiling, and headed back to Associated, the truck much lower and slower than the ride out, the gearbox crunching. We'd have to unload, then return the same afternoon to pick up the remainder of the cards.

When we got to the shop, Dad greeted me with a corned beef sandwich from Manny's and a Coke. While I had lunch in Dad's executive office, the men unloaded the truck and started the baling process.

"Great work," Dad said. "You done? Want to go home?"

"It wasn't my work, Dad. It was Bobby. He is the strongest man in the world. And Johnny is strong too and a wonderful driver."

I loved the morning. I wanted to go again. But Dad had had it. He wanted to go home, so we left for Glencoe and I missed my new camaraderie on the afternoon run back to the XYZ Corporation.

The next morning, we had two stops, one in the Loop and another somewhere on the West Side. The Loop stop was going to be tricky. We had to pick up the load in an alley. Johnny perfectly navigated the Loop's one-way streets without the aid of Siri or a GPS and parked us in front of the correct freight entrance. The truck was nearly as wide as the alley itself.

We got out of the cab and walked to the service entrance. Just as Johnny was about to pound on the door, a white guy down the dark alley yelled at us:

"Get that truck outta here! You're fucking blocking the alley."

He was a fat little guy with a no-nonsense look.

"We are trying to make a pickup here," Johnny told him.

"You are scavengers; get the fuck outta here," he repeated.

Johnny actually made eye contact with me and nodded in the guy's direction.

"Go on," he seemed to be saying. "You're Dan Friedman's son. You got this."

Johnny was not going to let us get blown off quite so easily.

I turned down the alley and walked towards the guy, outraged.

"We are not scavengers!" I told him. "We are a paper company. We are here to pick up a load."

"OK," he said. "Be quick about it!"

We took two or three filthy loads from an eighth-floor hallway down a low-capacity elevator and moved on, the little fat guy gone. It wasn't worth the trip. Then we headed west to another new data processing center in another industrial park and filled the balance of the truck with more cartons of freshly punched cards, the good stuff.

"Hey, Dad," I said when we got back. We'd had an interesting day and I wanted to tell him about it.

Dad was standing there on the loading dock in one of his yellow Brooks Brothers short-sleeved summer shirts, examining the load.

"That stuff you got this morning is garbage."

He was already expecting me to know the difference between good quality paper and bad. Should I have rejected that first load? Wasn't that Johnny's job?

I wanted to regale him with my story of vanquishing the guy in the alley, but I could tell he wasn't interested. No cash in moral victories. No such thing as a win if you don't get paid. Winners get paid. They don't pick up worthless scrap paper in an alley in downtown Chicago, however character-building they might find it.

It was readily apparent that I was of minimal help to Johnny and Bobby, but at least I wasn't a complete obstacle to their work. Johnny treated me like a fragile item that might break, and Bobby helped me heave boxes, but I was contributing at least some, I hoped.

The next day turned out to be one of the hottest of the summer. Every pickup took us to a different part of the city. Most of the waste paper we saw had been sitting somewhere for years covered in dust and mouse droppings. Also piled up in every location were boxes of vacuum tubes and transistors from early computers and pieces of old data processing machines, all worthless, according to Dad. It was rare to find a pure white load of high-quality paper. Almost every load we brought in was a mixed load of white and colored paper that needed hand sorting back at the shop.

Noble Johnny Crenshaw was master of our vehicle and the city streets. He never got lost, never made a wrong turn. In a different world, he'd have driven for UPS. He was another underdog king of Chicago, son of a Georgia sharecropper, as unheralded as Dad. Johnny and Dad had more in common than not. Both were up from nothing. That afternoon we get stuck in traffic on the southbound Dan Ryan, heading home in a heavy truck in the sweltering cab where Bobby and I had both fallen asleep.

Powerful, kind, and silent, Bobby was the person that most fascinated me in this world of my father's. We didn't exchange two words, but I was drawn to him and wished I knew more, wished I knew how to speak to him, wished I could help him in any small way like he helped me. During the winter months I'd continue to ask Dad about Bobby, and Dad thought I was absurd for asking. Dad did not even know Bobby's last name and had not the faintest personal interest in him or any of the men. Bobby, like the others, was a small, replaceable cog in an unreliable machine.

When I asked Dad what he paid Bobby, Dad turned on me fast.

"Are you kidding me? You're down here a week and already organizing my men? Is this what they teach you at New Trier? Get outta town!"

Dad was genuinely furious with me.

What a cruel world.

These were the days before federal oversight of workplace safety and cleanliness, before the creation of OSHA, the Occupational Safety and Health Administration. Dad sold Associated to a crony of his not long after Nixon created the agency. He thought the cost of regulations would hamper his operation and diminish his profit. Dad's factory floor would have failed every basic OSHA requirement. Some of Dad's men had no shoes, some openly drank on the job, the single toilet for the men was fouled, the place was badly lit, the air was unclean, an open elevator shaft loomed at the back of the dark building, and protective eyewear for factory workers had yet to become industry standard. Associated Salvage was a pre-OSHA success story. For better or worse, it could not exist today. It was built on the backs of low-paid black labor. Dad was extremely sensitive about this, but it's true, Dad. Johnny Crenshaw and E. B. Watson got paid, but all the other hands got peanuts and it did not matter if they left. They were simple laborers, the muscle. Associated was located in the middle of Chicago's vast and rapidly growing black belt at 4150 South Union Avenue. There were dozens more waiting in line for any job that became available. I watched eager young applicants turned away every day, always told by Jackie or my father, "Check back with us later, you never know."

After only a week of lifting boxes my body started to change, my arms and shoulders, as if by magic, getting bigger before my eyes. Standing shirtless in front of the mirror at home I liked what I saw. I was beginning to look a little tough. Despite this, Dad now decided to keep me in the shop. No more road trips for me. My new job was sorting cards, idiot-proof, the lowest rung on the totem pole at Associated Salvage, demoting me just as I was beginning to gain traction. Now I was watching from the sidelines as Johnny and Bobby, the cavaliers, leapt into the cab every morning and rode off together in search of adventure on the streets of Chicago.

That pissed me off. I liked being with the men. Johnny and Bobby were showing me how to be one. Dad said he was doing it for my safety, but that was baloney. I was sure that Dad was looking ahead. He did not want me getting too interested in Associated Salvage. He did not want South Union Avenue to be my future.

Still, driving to and from work with Dad in the big Cadillac was fun and unpredictable, detours always taken at the last second, Dad suddenly cutting across lanes of traffic to make a dangerous quick turn. He knew all kinds of people in the city, working in newsstands and gas stations, at dives and fancy joints. One morning he engaged in a long conversation with a man dressed in coveralls at the gas station and got back in the car.

"Who was that?" I asked.

"A cousin," he replied.

"We have a cousin who works at a gas station?"

"He owns eight."

Near Maxwell Street he waved at more guys from the car.

"Who are they?" I asked.

"More cousins," he told me.

We pulled into the West Side haberdasher called Benjamin and walked into the store. It was vast and well lit. A half-dozen Jewish tailors with tape measures draped around their necks were standing around looking like rabbis.

"Pick out anything you want," Dad told me with a wave of his hand.

"Well, honestly, Dad, I don't have a sports jacket. I could use a nice sports jacket to wear to the track." I had noted how the owners and trainers dressed, and I wanted to emulate them. They were my first style meisters.

He bought me a tweed sports coat which I wore to Arlington Park the following Saturday, a beautiful coat which fit for a year. I now had everything I needed at Arlington except my own thoroughbred, and I was lobbying for that.

Never on the phone at home, Dad was always on the phone at work, sometimes laughing, sometimes talking in hushed tones so I couldn't overhear anything he said. Some of his calls were business, some personal, I understood that.

One day driving home from work Dad suggested to me, in the nicest and most sensitive of ways, that if I would like to meet a woman to take care of me, to introduce me, as it were, well then, he could arrange that.

So, I was sixteen years old at the time and thought I was on the brink of getting laid myself, and that I did not need Dad's help on that score, but I told Dad thanks nonetheless, that I would think about it. But I wasn't stupid enough to reject the offer outright.

An important skill Dad and I had mastered by then was how to talk and listen to each another in such a way so as not to make either of us bolt from the room. Unlike other kids with no patience for their parents, I always listened carefully to him, considered what he had to say, and tried to never overreact.

This new Dad introducing himself for the first time today, however, was considerably more versatile and surefooted than the suburban Dad I knew in Glencoe, perhaps even more sparky than any dad out of Roald Dahl. Unlike Dahl's dads, my dad was a cosmopolitan dad who could unfurl before me the secrets of a vast metropolis. I liked this about him but was appalled that he wanted to mess with my sex life.

Working this offer over in my semi-developed teenage brain, I weighed the advantages and disadvantages as best I could. I knew that a boy being introduced to an experienced woman in this fashion was a sophisticated European concept, and I totally loved and admired Europe if only for this reason. But my next thought was what this meant about Dad, that he knew such women himself, and this hurt me, learning in this way that my father had been unfaithful to my beautiful mother. I did not like that at all. On the other hand, the idea turned me on. It stimulated me. I wanted to go for it. It could not be bad.

My degenerate, high-achieving friends from New Trier would assemble in my bedroom on Apple Tree Lane from time to time to shoot the shit and smoke some weed. These fellows are all miraculously still alive today, but they all left Chicago years ago for Boca Raton, Scottsdale, and the Keys. If they had remained in Chicago, they'd certainly all be dead. These guys were very smart and corruptible, and I liked them for both reasons. So I floated the still undigested idea over to them.

"Guys, my father offered to take me to a whore he knows in the city . . . what do you think? What would you do?"

"Your dad is so cool!" Epstein said right off the bat, jumping out of the chair. "Are you fucking kidding me? I wish my dad would do that for me!"

Nice response. My dad was cool. Okay. I'm good with that. Dahl's dads were duds compared with mine.

The other two jokers were confounded and stammered, too stoned for words. Pot and booze had only limited appeal to me. Like Dad, I wanted to be vigilant, alert, not incapacitated. We in our family valued knowing what was going on. A stoned Kasiel Skolnick, I know now, would never have made it on board the SS *Breslau*.

The pink, blue, and yellow IBM cards got sorted into one press, the white and cream-colored cards into the other. White cards with colored stripes went into the colored press. A twenty-pound carton of two thousand IBM punch cards might contain ten or twenty colored cards inserted randomly into the neat row of white cards. These, maddeningly, had to be removed by hand and dropped into the colored card press. This was imperative. We could not sell a three-ton bale of white paper to the mill up in Appleton or Stevens Point with even a few colored cards accidentally dropped in. Such an error would come back to discredit and haunt the Associated Salvage Company.

In those years, I never paid my father the respect he deserved. I could never have run a company like this myself, much less have invented it. But at his back he always heard the baleful cries of poverty and woe from the Marks Nathan Home, and that was what drove him every morning to 4150 South Union Avenue.

The pathetic fact was, I wasn't good at sorting cards, either. I quickly lost patience removing the few colored cards from the thousands of boxes stacked up waiting for me to sort them, my hands were bleeding, shredded by paper, so I ended up indiscriminately dumping boxes of mostly white cards into the white press, just flipping the entire box over and dumping them in. Looking down into the press I could see the accusatory colored cards spread out at the bottom, staring up at me, telling me I was an idiot.

Jackie watched the floor like a hawk. When he saw what I was doing, tossing colored cards into the white card press, he actually jumped into the bottom of the press and picked them all out one by one and held them up to my face in his fist.

"You do not, ever, throw colored cards in with the white. I thought I told you that."

Jackie was furious with me. If I was a *swartza* I'd have been fired on the spot, but I wasn't a *swartza;* I was the boss's son, and fireproof.

Dad and I were bound together that summer. I was his willing student at Associated Salvage during the week, his *Racing Form* analyst at Arlington Park on Saturday, and his golf partner on Sunday at the Highland Park Country Club.

The *Rules of Golf* is a 180-page document that Dad never read. He had no prior experience in the sport. There was no golf club anywhere near the Marks Nathan Home. No one in the orphanage owned golf clubs or played golf. Boxers and baseball players were their sports heroes, not golfers. When Dad first started playing, he was seeing the golf course and figuring it out as he went.

We would arrive at the club without a tee time ("what's a tee time?") on the busiest day of the week and somehow force ourselves to the front of the long queue, ignoring the insults and protests of other golfers patiently waiting their turn. How he did this I do not exactly remember. I'm sure I blocked it out, because I knew in my heart, even with no experience in the game, that cutting in front of all these guys could not be correct. There was never any waiting with Dad. Decorum was not one of his strong suits. Dad did not get where he was in life by waiting in line for anyone, that's the way he saw it.

We'd tee off on the first hole in front of many irate golfers, Dad, a leftie, always swinging way too fast, a blur, snap-hooking his drive far off to the right, over by the third hole, the ball barely getting airborne, a hot, low line drive. After completing the first hole ten or twelve shots later, Dad would stop and scan the horizon. He did not believe, or had not learned, that golf holes were designed to be played in order, one through eighteen. Dad saw a congested golf course as he would a traffic jam on the Edens Expressway, and it was his right to drive around it.

Usually all the holes on Sunday, like every other summer weekend, were packed with foursomes. But Dad would look across to the faraway sixth hole, which was empty. If we could quickly drive past all the golfers on two, three, four, and five, we would have six to ourselves, which was exactly what we'd do.

Dad had his own name for this brand of golf. He called it "zig-zagging."

"Let's zig-zag," he would tell me with a grin.

We would zig-zag our way across the entire golf course, angering golfers on every hole, gesturing at us with their fist or middle finger, playing number one, six, seven, and nine, then thirteen, fifteen, and eighteen, either quitting at that point or going back to play two, three, four, and five. Dad was a terrible golfer. I was a terrible golfer. Neither of us had had any golf instruction, but we were even worse at golf etiquette, which is why we had no friends at Highland Park Country Club. Dad acknowledged no etiquette of any sort in any setting.

Any of the more established, prestigious Jewish clubs on the North Shore would have booted Dad out, or not admitted him in the first place, and I would not have blamed them, but his conduct was not atypical of the membership at HPCC, made up of first-generation Jews and Italians who were rough-cut, funny, and loud. I recall one guy's son brought his own lunch in a brown paper bag into the club dining room every Sunday, which my father, now a snob, found abhorrent. No one ever called Dad out on his behavior because they were afraid of him. They thought he was crazy, maybe a little dangerous. The fact was, he just didn't know the rules. He was either too impatient to study them or too proud to ask.

Dad eventually settled down, learned the civilizing rituals of golf, submitted to the gentle leadership of the club pro, took many lessons from him which he enjoyed, played the holes in correct sequence, and became part of a regular foursome. This was a big win. Dad actually worked hard at his golf game and became a decent golfer, capable of legitimately breaking ninety a half-dozen times a year. He enjoyed the game until the season when all the men in his foursome suddenly died, one after the other, men all in their mid-fifties. Dad lost his entire golfing foursome in the summer of 1972, and after that, golf was not the same for him. He loved those guys and kept a photograph on his bedside table of the four of them in colorful golf attire on the first tee of the Highland Park Country Club.

―――

My three-week paid internship at Associated Salvage Company was coming to an end; I was going back to join the young socialists at left-wing New Trier High School. Thank God. Only three weeks of work on the South Side of Chicago with my father and I was ready to reclaim my life as a suburban high school kid. The following summer I'd spend in San Francisco enrolled in classes at Menlo College, going to strip clubs in North Beach, and becoming friends with a fast group from Beverly Hills High School who taught me a great deal about sartorial splendor, English sports cars, hashish, and California girls. Few of those guys are still alive.

When school resumed in September, I spent less time with Dad but still hovered over his shoulder in the evenings while he did the math. I'd stretch out on his bed engulfed in his strong scent and read the sports section while he did calculations from the Eames lounger. WFMT was always on in the background, the dulcet tones of Norm Pellegrini introducing pieces by Berlioz or Bizet. Norm Pellegrini, Phil Georgeff, Jack Brickhouse, Irv Kupcinet, Dick Biondi, and Studs Terkel were the voices from my Chicago childhood.

By now, Dad had accumulated investable sums and became a self-taught financier in the bond and stock market. He had a Merrill Lynch broker whom he abused with insults and ridicule over the phone. Dad used this guy as a contraindicator and trusted no judgment but his own. The broker was simply "an order taker."

Dad first became obsessed with the intricacies of the municipal bond market, the creditworthiness of remote, unheard-of bond issuing agencies, and believed from the bottom of his heart that double tax-free income was one of life's greatest rewards. The sock drawer in his bedroom bureau became stuffed with bearer bonds from small cities across America whose balance sheets Dad had studied with the intensity of a microbiologist searching for a cure for Ebola. Dad would talk out loud about interest rates, share with me his thinking, and show me evidence to support his theories.

I always got it, immediately. If you hear your father talking out loud for years about municipal bonds, you absorb that arcane knowledge in your bones.

Building on his foundation of munis, Dad moved into stocks. These were the days of the nifty fifty, but Dad was interested in more esoteric instruments. He told me that bonds were for security and stocks for speculation, not the coupon.

"Who can get excited about AT&T?" he'd utter with contempt.

Following Gulf+Western became one of his chief obsessions and forms of entertainment, and Charlie Bluhdorn was one of those guys who received Dad's rambling, drug-fueled, late-night missives. Bluhdorn was a deal-maker on a scale that staggered Dad's imagination. He invented a whole new genre: the conglomerate.

These markets, with intricacies and moving parts to captivate his hyperactive intelligence, even more so than the completely unique scrap paper business, were made for Dad. He was way out ahead of it all. He read everything, attended annual shareholder meetings in Loop hotels, to which he dragged me, picked the brains of the most successful men he met, and everywhere encountered only ignorance, "dummies," as he called them. Dad was combative and supremely arrogant, always the smartest guy in the room. He told me to pick a stock for him to buy in order to further involve and educate me. I selected a local Chicago company, Consolidated Foods, which became Sara Lee. This was one of the great dud stocks of all time. It put me to sleep. The original $40 share price grew to $73 after a decade.

Dad then started aggressively trading futures and options and became fascinated with the operation of the Chicago Board of Trade, where the real money was made. Here he lost me. I understood all of it but not options. Dad believed that the Chicago Board of Trade was his true calling, and he was right. The sums were greater, the risks were higher, the action nonstop. The ambience stirred his blood. It kept his central nervous system on high alert. Trading made him feel alive. It was addictive, like gambling. He offered to buy me a seat on the exchange, I should become a trader, he suggested. He should buy a seat for himself, I thought.

"Let's go downtown and watch the action," he said, trying to entice me.

This was an enormous proposition for a kid still in eleventh grade. Not understanding futures and options and working at the Board of Trade might not be a great combination, I thought. Dad wanted me to follow in his footsteps but I wasn't sure I could follow him there, or wanted to. We had two young traders living on Apple Tree Lane by then; both drove noisy Porsches, and both looked unsmiling and unhappy. Traders stared into the face of ruin every day, I knew that much. They looked miserable for a reason. One false step and they were done. Shooting hoops in our driveway, I saw one of them come home during market hours and leave his black 911 in the flowerbed. He missed his entire driveway. He fell out of the car into the shrubs, left the car door open, and weaved through the front door of his house, slamming it shut. That was Mr. Berman, the trader. He lost everything before lunch and wasn't happy about it. Dad thought Berman should pick himself up, scrape together a few dollars, and go back to the pits. Dad thought huge losses were a part of the game, the way to earn your *cojones*. I told Dad my *cojones* were perfect as is.

With my unpredictable dad, there was often something strange happening, and I learned to take it all in stride. One night, for a *meshuggeneh* reason all his own—maybe it was the potent cocktail of pharmaceuticals never fully flushed from his system—my father became furious with me, and in the hallway between our bedrooms, squared off like a boxer, raised his fists, and blew smoke from his nostrils, ready to fight me. This was my father at his most unhinged, reverting to his ten-year-old self, facing one of his first demons from the Marks Nathan Home. By this time, I was seventeen and much larger and stronger than he. I squared off too and, with a complete calm that surprised me, quickly sized up my father and knew how badly I could hurt him. I saw so clearly I could punch through his defenses and with one blow break his jaw or his nose. I saw exactly where I'd land my shot. Instead, I went outside in a fury where his Coupe de Ville was parked in the driveway, and I delivered that punch, intended for him, into the driver's side door, breaking my knuckles and denting the car. Through the pain, it was gratifying to see the size of the mark I left. This was no lightweight Toyota. It was a big sheet metal 1968 Cadillac, which Dad drove around with a dent in the door until he got a new car the following spring. This episode was just more proof to me that I was fully and truly his son, as mercurial and potentially explosive as he.

Here are a few small lessons I learned from the poor *schlemiel* from the Marks Nathan Home, the man who did not know how to be a father because he did not have one himself: tell the truth, omit nothing, carry no burden, carry no shame. I learned this from him because he could not tell the truth about himself, and the sense of disgrace he carried about his past fueled but also handicapped him. Define yourself anew every day, I learned watching him. No one owes you a living, this he hammered home. Except for a handful of people, if you are lucky to have even that many, you are completely on your own. Hard work is the cornerstone of it all. Show up early, work for yourself, work around the clock, work at night, always work, get your hands dirty. Take reasoned, educated risks. Don't bet it all on one horse in one race. Investing in the future is what is called "being paid on the come." Dinner at a Michelin three-star restaurant is not worth the price because your appetite always returns within a few hours. Get to the airport early and go straight to the gate, to make sure it's there. Tip a couple of bucks, but make it a big deal by slapping the cash into the recipient's hand. Pay attention all the time to every detail going on around you. All that fatherhood requires is abundant love. In music, art, and human interaction, passion is everything. Always hug and kiss your best male friends without hesitation, especially the ones who cringe when you kiss them. Never miss the chance to tell your children that you love them. You can break the mold completely and abandon Judaism, but years later you can come back to it, as he did. You can have many careers, not just one, and be successful at them all. Women are beautiful. Resilience and determination are everything. The world is full of wonderful places, but no place is better than Chicago. Having him and learning all this from him, I did the best I could. He opened my heart and mind to every possibility. Uneducated, with no father of his own save his loving brother Sol, he taught me everything he knew.

Seven

University Circle

There was much Dad could not help me with after I got married and left Chicago. Seeing the writing on the wall, my mother's blessing for me on my wedding day was a downer: "I hope you have ten good years." Ten good years was about what we had, but the great news is, I'm still alive. I ended up, implausibly, in the South, in Charlottesville, because I married my college sweetheart, both of us age twenty-one, and moved to be near her family. She was born in a coal town on the Ohio River in West Virginia where we were married in her mother's living room.

From West Virginia, Charlottesville was a significant step up. But we married, had children, and settled down. It was a quiet, safe, pretty place to raise a family. In Charlottesville, I published magazines, became the municipal bond guy for the local branch of a global investment firm, renovated old buildings and houses, wrote fiction and nonfiction, taught writing at the local university, played a lot of golf, and cherished every second of my fatherhood.

My dad was a big fan of the magazines, and he loved my writing. Thank god he lived to see some of it. I have in my possession one of those famous, urgent, late-night, sleeping pill–induced letters of his, in this case written to me, dated September 25, 1981. It is vintage Dad. In it he writes:

Dear Son,

I must tell you something. Your magazine [*Albemarle*] arrived and as you say it is the best yet. Let me explain something. As you know, I have accomplished very little in my life. Oh sure, I made a decent living. But I never had pride in my work. It was a means to an end. But when I read your cover story ["Here in the Honeysuckle"] I was filled with pride and love. Genes are unreal. You know my high school annual [Lindblom, 1932, Dad looking dapper in a navy blue double-breasted suit for his class photo, wearing round eyeglasses like I. M. Pei] indicated I wanted to be a writer. But obviously I couldn't because my education was so limited.

But I read the story and your words, phrases and thoughts jump out at me and I say to myself: My God! I wanted to write that personally but it would be impossible. I couldn't do it. I can read a profit and loss statement, a bank statement, a proxy, but my true love writing what you have written is beyond me. My god, how can you get excited baling and looking at a bale of wastepaper?

You are sentimental, emotional, understanding and caring. Thank goodness you are doing what you are happy with and let me tell you if I could write that would be my same style.

Life is beautiful when you see your son evolve to the style the father (illiterate) aspired to. You make my life fulfilled. I love you for it.

Thanks and love,
Neurotic Dad

My true love writing, Dad writes to me.
Genes are unreal, he says. It's true.
Life is beautiful.... Thanks, Dad.

These are the only words I have left from him. I had a pair of his gold-plated cufflinks embossed with his initials, DRF, but I lost one twenty years ago, and the orphan still rattles around in my jewelry box. I have no audiotape of him. All I have left is this letter, a handful of faded photographs, and his high school annual, *The Eagle,* from Lindblom, 1932.

To know that my father was on my side in this most cherished pursuit meant everything to me. He could have criticized my departure from Chicago and the work I chose, but he didn't. Support from him meant the world. What child could say that his father, especially from such a tough background, gave him the green light to paint, compose music, write stories, or dream dreams for a living? Not just that, but to tell me, in the process, that I was also fulfilling his highest ambition for himself? I have kept this letter close to me, in my desk drawer, among my most precious valuables, inside a favorite book, since I received it. I handle it with great care because in it, my father's soul is connecting with mine.

This letter crystallized the highest qualities I most adored about my father, the ones that endure with me now: his modesty, generosity, and self-effacement, his understatement and pride in creating wealth, his instinct to put his son before himself, which is exactly how I learned to put my son before me. Giving your son lots of headroom to top you in life was a lesson I learned from him, although I left my son more room than my father left me. Saying goodbye to Dad and Chicago by moving across the country when I was young and newly married was just something one did at that stage of life, but I missed him terribly. We swore to each other that we'd talk as often as we could.

The small sect of Jews I encountered in rural Virginia included the tweediest members of the local foxhunting crowd, right out of a Jane Austen drawing room, even if they moved there from New Jersey. Many gelded their Jewish names and remade their history, deleting the entire Jewish part. Many tried to wash off their Jewishness, if only they could scrub hard enough. Shape-shifting to suit the uptight local scene, to fit in, was de rigueur for everyone, Jews and non-Jews alike. I did it too, wearing khakis and logoed golf shirts, getting *goyim* enough to join the country club and be invited to the parties hosted by Missy and Landon. I even ditched my very flashy, beloved Jewish

Porsche Turbo with whale tail for the prestige vehicle of choice thereabouts: a huge Suburban, good for driving kids to school and over gravel roads to visit friends who lived way out in scenic tick and copperhead country. We bought a majestic, run-down red brick mansion on University Circle against my parents' wishes, a magically beautiful place but a renovation nightmare, and I lived there for thirty-five years, alone with the Labrador the last several years after she moved out.

Dad always tried his best to be a good sport whenever he and Mom came to visit. I was enthusiastic about Charlottesville and saw potential in it for my young family, but Dad looked around, found nothing to engage him, raised his expressive eyebrows and wrinkled his mighty forehead, as if to say: "I don't get it. What in the world are you doing here?" Thankfully, his manners were good enough not to say so out loud in the company of my bride, who loved our new home. We'd take Dad to parties over the Christmas holidays, and I'd watch his demeanor as he worked the room. He wasn't impressed with the precious plantation houses and their occupants. He loved rooting out the truth in these situations, getting to the absolute bottom of it, always knowing that what you witness in such cases is often complete fiction.

On the way home after one enormously dressy dinner party, he told me, like Sherlock Holmes announcing a discovery: "Your friend is a complete fraud. *Weinstock* is the real name, not *Wentworth*. His grandfather was from the Lower East Side of New York, grew up in a tenement on

Rivington Street, started out as a peddler with a pushcart in the rag business, that's how your friend got that big house of his."

We exploded with laughter about it, the charade and vanity of it all, a constant source of merriment for us.

"*Derrière la façade*," I said.

And there was a big façade. In fact, it was almost all façade, a complete stage set.

People in Charlottesville consider funerals as they would garden parties. So-and-so's funeral was "very, very well-done," someone would say, while another funeral was "a mess." In all my years there, I never understood the difference between a good funeral and a bad one, and why it mattered.

The fact was, I made a huge mistake that would cost me. By moving to Virginia and buying in, I quietly exchanged my vibrant, if chaotic, life in Chicago for hers in nearby West Virginia, and in doing so, lost touch with *my* Chicago, my father and mother, all my cousins, all my old friends, and who I really was. I pushed aside my defining religious conflict, Jew or Gentile, and went with my wife's family to church. My vast family network in Chicago, Glencoe, and the Jewish community; our history with the Marks Nathan Home and Associated Salvage—all of it—I wish I'd shared more of this with my children instead of pushing their mother's Waspy ways.

"You can't send me to Treblinka! I'm with those Wasps!" I must have been thinking all those years.

They were certainly going to shield me with their lives in the event of another Holocaust.

So in 2014, finally unencumbered, no wife, no house, all the mahogany furniture given away, the brass trivets and Jefferson cups discarded, I moved back to Chicago in an effort to retrieve at least some of what I'd left there. Life was turning out to be generous and long enough to allow me time to correct some of my errors, omissions, and missteps.

My son Nat, born in Charlottesville, was my father's first grandson and the great-grandson of the brave Kasiel Skolnick. With these two iconoclasts on his patrilineal side, my hopes for Nat were high. Dad loved Nat and studied him, looking for clues to his future, but my father died in February 1988, when his grandson was only nine years old, and missed out on almost everything.

Nat showed signs of math aptitude from early childhood. He began writing code at age five. He dismantled household appliances "to see how they are put together." His sixth grade SAT scores were in the 99th percentile of all college-bound twelfth graders. He became a National Merit Scholar and National Science Scholar and went to MIT. In his East Campus dorm room, he started a software company after traveling to Mexico City to meet Miguel de Icaza, his future partner and kindred spirit. The company they created thrived, and in three years they sold it to a larger company listed on NASDAQ. I have to think that Kasiel Skolnick of Knyszyn and Dan Friedman of Marks Nathan had a hand in this.

When I visit Nat in San Francisco, as I do now once or twice a year, and drop in on him at his office on Pacific Avenue up from the Embarcadero, I think first of my father in any of his customary poses, in our box at Arlington Park, on the loading dock at Associated Salvage, driving his Cadillac to work with his great head hanging over the steering wheel, scribbling calculations on the back of an envelope, and the ecstasy he would feel seeing Nat like this. Dad would understand all he has done, that it was not by chance, that luck was not involved. I am telling you, Dad, wherever you are in that big car of yours, look down upon your grandson, look at us now.

Nat is Kasiel without the looming threat of the next pogrom, my father unencumbered by an impoverished, fatherless childhood. Nat also had me around, not always perfect, but as good a father as I could be, having learned a lot about fatherhood from my own.

Today, Nat is on the phone in his office, in jeans, blue suede running shoes, and a tailored cotton shirt, stretched out in his Herman Miller chair, listening intently, speaking to his lawyer with the fewest number of words. An enormous amount is at stake but his demeanor is completely chill. I love seeing him like this. I love being with him. In the elevator going up to his office, young computer engineers look at me and say, "You must be Nat's dad! You and he look so much alike."

Kasiel died in 1916, my father survived the Marks Nathan Home, I survived my father. It's been a circuitous, sometimes dangerous route, but all of us are connected. Four generations of Friedman men lined up in my mind in the same photograph, or standing on each other's shoulders, one luckier and taller than the one that came before. This is our Chicago Jewish American family portrait: Kasiel, 5'1", born in 1881; my father Dan, 5'8", born in 1915; me, 6'1", if I stand properly, born in 1951; and Nat at 6'3", fourteen inches taller than Kasiel, born in 1977.

My grandfather hit the streets of Chicago in that lucky year, 1903, changed his name, and fathered six children before his death in 1916. My father's early years were extremely dire. I lived in a true Golden Age overseen by a golf-loving president who had a tree named after him at Augusta.

The only threat to my existence was Vietnam, and I would have gone had I been drafted. I was nineteen years old in the 1971 draft lottery and drew number 326. The number of young Americans dying in Vietnam was falling by 1971, but casualties were still enormous. Had I drawn number 150 or lower I would have arrived in time for the terrible quagmire of Dewey Canyon II; Lam Son, the largest helicopter assault of the war with nearly seven hundred US helicopters destroyed or damaged; the return to Khe Sanh; and the Christmas bombing of Hanoi. I watched it all on television thinking, my God, that could have been me, dying there, save for drawing a lucky number.

I can only conjecture what my father and grandfather might have achieved had they been born into Nat's world. To Kasiel and my father I say: you did everything within your power for us. You studied the terrain and laid a mighty structure for us to build upon. Beloved father and grandfather, we thank and honor you.

May his great name be blessed, forever and ever. Blessed, praised, glorified, exalted, extolled, honored, elevated and lauded be the Name of the holy one. Blessed is he—above and beyond any blessings and hymns. Praises and consolations which are uttered in the world; and say Amen. May there be abundant peace from Heaven, and life, upon us and upon all Israel; and say Amen.

—*The Mourner's Kaddish*

Eight

Lake Shore Drive

One of the first things I did after moving back to Chicago and settling into Lake Shore Drive was take myself to 1550 South Albany Avenue and pay my first visit to the Marks Nathan Home. The West Side of Chicago had changed a lot over the years. The United Center had taken the place of the Chicago Stadium, and the West Loop had been turned into one of the best fine-dining districts in the city. When I took my youngest daughter to dinner at Girl & the Goat, I refused to get out of the cab until the restaurant entrance was in sight. She thought that was absolutely hysterical. West Randolph Street was a no-go zone in my youth. Now it's full of Michelin-starred restaurants. I had been away that long.

But as I got closer and closer to the Home on South Albany, vestiges of the old West Side, the West Side that I knew, came into focus—long lines at soup kitchens, authentically shabby people (not hipsters), billboards for sufferers from bedbugs, clusters of men in empty lots warming themselves by glowing braziers, yellow police tape surrounding an entire city block where a shooting had taken place the night before. Just nineteen minutes by car from Lake Shore Drive, South Albany Avenue is the pit of Chicago, bypassed by waves of urban renewal.

There I was, sixty-four years old, going to the Marks Nathan Home for the first time. I had never seen the place, never been taken there, never driven past it with my dad. There it was, completely intact, looking exactly as it did in its vintage photographs, across the street from Douglas Park where the city now runs a summer music event called "Riot Fest." The huge, block-long building looked un-rehabilitated, distressed, and haunted.

"Dad," I recall asking him many times, "where is the Home? Please take me there so that I can see it."

These exchanges frequently took place in the front seat of one of his 1960s Coupe de Villes, where all of our important talking took place.

"Are you crazy?" he would ask, turning his huge head towards me with that look of sheer incredulity, his son a complete fool. "Why would I ever want to show you that?"

True. It was not exactly me showing my kids Glencoe and New Trier. But at least it could have been a starting point for a conversation, part of my education.

I parked the flawless white 911S in front of the Home and locked it. Two Chicago police cruisers were parked in front of the crime scene one block up the street, their uniformed occupants taking notes on the murder from the night before, the crime earning less than an inch of type in that morning's *Trib*. No one asked me what I was doing there in that neighborhood in that car. No one even looked at me. I stood and stared at the building, trying to imagine my father as a five-year-old boy running down the sidewalk. Douglas Park looked as bleak as it did in that 1920 family photograph, the sole vestige of Dad's childhood, which I have on my bookcase: Jenny and her orphans. Then I walked to the front door of the Marks Nathan Home and let myself in.

The place is now called Sacred Heart Home, and it is an institution for the insane. It scores among the lowest of all such institutions in the city of Chicago based on objective criteria such as cleanliness, number of professional staff per resident, quality of nursing care, bedbug count, and so forth. According to one survey, over 80 percent of its 154 residents are being administered antipsychotic drugs. This is where my father spent his childhood, a tarnished plaque affixed near the front door says so, a purpose-built orphanage for Orthodox Jewish children turned into a storage facility for the impoverished and deranged. This building has been housing broke, mad, and disenfranchised people since 1912.

Nursing homes are reviewed on websites as commonly, and scathingly, as restaurants and hotels. Sacred Heart Home scores one star (out of five) for overall quality. A visitor notes "puddles of urine in the stairwells," and another comments, "it could certainly use some cleaning." One star seemed very generous to me.

Inside the front door I found a reception check-in desk and, just beyond that, a second door of thick glass through which I could see three or four patients mingling, some looking wild or hyperactive, flailing their arms, in a well-lit corridor. This second door was double-locked and bolted. A receptionist flanked by a security type in civilian clothes immediately looked up and asked if she could help. I told her that my father had lived as an orphan in this building for many years, and that I would like to tour the place. She told me that that was impossible, that Sacred Heart was a high-security facility, the public were not allowed inside. She told me to call the hospital administrator if I had further questions. I told her I'd called the administrator twice asking to see the place but never got a reply. The security guy stepped forward.

"Yeah, no one can just come in here," he said.

One look at the chaos on the other side of the thick glass door, and I decided I agreed with him. Wasn't sure I needed to go in there. After sixty-four years, however, I wasn't going to be dismissed so quickly.

"Do you know this was an orphanage for Jewish children?" I asked him. "Have you seen the plaque by the front door? Does anyone like me with connections to the Marks Nathan Home ever come here, like I am doing today? Can you please tell me a little about the place? Is the building falling apart? How long have you worked here?"

His name was Taye, and he had worked at the Sacred Heart Home for eleven years. He was not unpleasant. He understood the purpose of my surprise visit. He and the receptionist relaxed a little when they determined I wasn't an inspector of some sort or a lunatic. No, he said, no one had ever come to the building with questions about its history as an orphan home, at least not during his tenure. There were no vestiges or remains of the former orphanage inside the building. The plaque on the front door was the only evidence that the Home had ever existed on that site.

The receptionist added that, despite appearances, the one-hundred-and-two-year-old building was "in good shape." Its only remaining original features, she volunteered, were the dark red granite terrazzo floors and the brick façade. The large attached synagogue on the south side of the building, where my father attended Hebrew school, where Sol sang as Home cantor, was "not in use." That was about all they could tell me.

Taye walked me outside. He had a tough enough job maintaining order at Sacred Heart Home without me showing up requesting an interview. I could tell he wanted to be nice, but also clearly wanted me to leave. In his unstated opinion, I wasn't as bad as the residents locked inside, but close.

Part of me relaxed, satisfied. I had exorcised a demon. It was worse than I could have imagined, but I had survived it. I finally overcame my fear and saw the Marks Nathan Home with my own eyes. I sensed my father there as a child, "wee Danny Friedman." That view of Douglas Park from the front steps of the Home was the same view he saw. I experienced a sliver of what he experienced by being there. I could imagine him running into the building over the worn red terrazzo. There was not much more I could do.

After one year in the Mies building in Chicago, I finally felt free of the detritus and filigree of old Virginia, its heavy crown molding and draperies, its porcelain Chinese import dogs adorning the mantelpiece and hearth, kitsch of the Old South. My blunt Chicago accent, always lurking beneath the surface, sprang back, too, as if I had never left the joint. No longer needing to gentrify my speech with *y'all* this and that, no longer needing to wear sweaters embroidered with the crossed swords of the state university or crest of the country club in order to show I belonged, I could now walk, talk, and dress any way I wished. For me, it helped that there was a critical mass of Jews in Chicago, still a minority, but a big Jewish presence. All these familiar, unknown Jews on the sidewalks and elsewhere helped me feel like I belonged in this city among them. I felt less sense of unease, less fear of rejection, less self-consciousness. Much less likelihood here of getting buttonholed at a cocktail party and being asked to explain my origins or something the Knesset might be planning. In Chicago, I wasn't a weird species. Here I was just another Jew. What a relief. I no longer needed to wallpaper or window-dress my "otherness."

Adjusting to the city, however, took time. Those first few weeks back felt like landing on the moon, in a place that bore some resemblance to the place I knew, but with all the people lost or missing, including my mother and father, all long gone. The truth is, I found a few of the old people, but I found many new ones, too.

I found Kasiel and my father reincarnated in Gregory, in Glenn's son Dan, and in my cousin Lynne's son Jordan. Of my three children, my daughter Victoria most fits this physical and energetic type. At a reunion bringing them together, they'd have no trouble seeing themselves in each other, or in Kasiel, the founder of our family. This I find gratifying.

Certain things about the city have not changed. As much as before, I admire the raffish, cosmopolitan charm of men and women out on the town on Rush Street or in the Gold

Coast. A large, well-done abstract painting, with the wonderful Chicago title *Passion, Sex, and Corruption* is offered for sale in a gallery window on Oak Street, and suddenly I covet it. I like the pale silver, slate-colored sky that hangs over the city, the lake, the horizon, and the city grid that goes on forever. I like the fact that Chicagoans are outgoing people who shout at one another, from across the street or in small groups. I like the way the shills in locally produced television ads, whether they're selling cars or pizza or flooring, always shout, especially the restaurateurs shouting about the superior conviviality of their establishments, sweat clinging to their foreheads. Chicago shills are a special breed. I have always liked the locally produced television jingles. And I love the *Tribune,* with America's most malicious sports writers. None of these details have changed since my childhood. And like Erik Larson, I love Chicago best in the cold. Winter is my favorite time of year.

Marsha Raynes is a licensed clinical social worker and the Director of the Chicago Jewish Adoption Network in Skokie, the first person, after Susan Baron, I contacted to help me discover and understand the details of my father's history in the Marks Nathan Home. We communicated via email, then I drove to Skokie to visit her in her office. Before our meeting, Marsha asked to see copies of my father's death certificate and my driver's license, to make sure I was who I told her I was.

When we sat down, Marsha handed over a sheaf of documents pertaining to my father's enrollment in the Home, material, some of it shocking, which I had never seen and never knew, including his intake form and questionnaire signed by Jenny; the results of Jenny's interview with the Home administrator; data about Jenny's income, work history, family, and places of residence during my father's Home years; Dad's letter of acceptance to the Home; his letter of discharge six years later; and his birth certificate. Dad was born as "Dan Friedman," not "Daniel Richard Friedman." He was Dan, never Daniel, the middle name was an add-on in later years, and he was born January 4, not January 1, as he always told us. He was born at home, 5520 South Halsted Street, delivered by a midwife from the nearby Presbyterian Hospital. Dad had a minor surgery of some sort at Mount Sinai Hospital January 15, 1922, age seven. The Friedman orphans in these documents were called Sollie, Annie, Minnie, Izzy, Simon, and Dan. His father's cause of death, again, was listed as "pneumonia" on two pages and as "pulmonary tuberculosis" on a third page.

Marsha knew I was coming to see her because my father omitted telling me the salient details of his childhood, and that simply, finally, I had to know a few things about him. She agreed that I had a right to his information. She had examined the documents and was ready to help me in any way she could. I was grateful to her.

"Secrets bring shame," Marsha told me.

"The conventional wisdom was that children didn't need to know certain things. But secrets are toxic. It was a convention at the time not to tell people they were adopted. I understand why people make the decisions they make. I am hoping that finding this material helps you with that."

"Thank you," I told her.

"Hold onto how successful your dad was, how he turned around a hard life and became a loving father to you. Hold onto all the blessings and his success. And especially, his amazing resilience.

"I am hoping," she continued, "finding this information helps you with that."

There was one last terrible question I had, one that carried enormous weight for me. I had to ask about my father's whispered, half-remembered comment, in the shadows between our bedrooms one night, that his father, Sam, in fact died of syphilis, which, if true, might well have been the reason no one ever spoke of him, and why he laid for nearly one hundred years in an unmarked grave.

"How am I to understand what my father said to me that night?" I asked her. "Is this a false memory or could it be true? Is this the reason Jenny was cast out, unprotected by her large family in Chicago? Was my father left to fend for himself in the Marks Nathan Home for a hushed-up misdeed of his father?"

Fifty million people died from the flu worldwide between 1916 and 1919, so his death from influenza was a likely cause, not at all implausible. The children of syphilitics were often born with terrible deformities. My father and his siblings were not. But I had to air out this last secret I had carried far too long.

"It is possible," she said, "but you will just never know. Syphilis in its later stages could lead to pneumonia or a lung condition like tuberculosis. It makes sense that the immediate cause of death be listed, even if the condition was caused by syphilis. Listing syphilis as a cause of death was often avoided by physicians in this way."

"But," she continued, "you really have no way of knowing if syphilis played a part in your grandfather's death. What impacted your family was a vague sense of shame around your grandfather, whether justified or not, and the fact that his closest family members never spoke of him after his death.

"But the fact is, you will just never know."

Greg and I talked this over and we agreed with her assessment. We understood the story of Kasiel, and all of the pieces finally fell into place. We knew who our grandfather was, where he had come from, how he'd gotten to Chicago, and his real name. We saw ourselves in him. He brought us to America where we would thrive. Yes, there were some things about him we would just never know, and we were OK with that.

In my transition, not long after my move back to Chicago, I started having recurrent dreams about home, even though I was happy in my new Chicago home.

"I want to go home," I said to myself in the dream.

I wanted to go home, and I did not know where to go. I was an old man, and I could not find my way. I had forgotten where my home was, or never had one to begin with. Maybe the beggars and street people I met on Michigan Avenue saying they are homeless had influenced my dreams. Like them, I was homeless, too.

My father and Chicago had called me. My decision to move back to Chicago after an absence of thirty-eight years was to reconnect with whatever "home" still meant; maybe it meant "hope." I feel most at home in Chicago, most proudly and instantaneously Chicagoan, the moment I get off any flight at O'Hare Airport, gateway to the giant city. The Helmut Jahn terminal always makes me feel like I have arrived there.

Another reason I wanted to return home to Chicago became obvious after that first year or so. Finally, I needed to end the debate, the charade, the ambivalence between my two sides, Jewish and Catholic. I was ready to choose, and I chose the Jews. Dad was conflicted about Jews and Judaism, but he was a Jew and nothing else. By choosing Chicago I chose him. Chicago, Kasiel's city, the city of my father, was the place to reclaim myself. That was it.

After much thought and trepidation, I made an appointment to meet Rabbi Edwin Goldberg at Temple Sholom, a large, historic Reform synagogue on Lake Shore Drive within a short drive of my island of Miesian serenity. Maybe I was going to add something to my vastly scaled-down life, stripped of all the furniture and accessories I had sold or given away. Maybe I was going to add faith.

Rabbi Goldberg was a tall, good-looking, nattily attired gentleman with a welcoming smile and cultivated demeanor. His fourth-floor office was spacious and lined with books, like the chairman of an English department or a dean's office in the Ivy League. He has already been tipped off by his assistant that I was a badly lapsed, highly conflicted Jew-Gentile who had never found any clergy willing to take me on, rejected by Jews and non-Jews alike, with enough confusion and hurt feelings to last several lifetimes. The Rabbi's assistant had scheduled the meeting to last just thirty minutes, which made me think three things: (1) he wasn't going to fire me in half an hour, (2) he had heard such tales of woe as mine and knew how to handle them, and (3) my chances for a positive outcome from this meeting were outstanding.

Rabbi Goldberg indicated a seat with a sweep of his hand and I dove right in.

"Rabbi, may I tell you a quick story?" I asked him.

"Yes, of course."

As I spoke, I felt like I was becoming my father. I knew I looked like him, coiled up like a ball ready to spring, and talked like him, too—like a machine gun, spitting out words with a sense of urgency akin to one of Dad's crazy late-night letters to gurus and great men. He was my father, after all.

"My paternal grandfather was named Kasiel Skolnick," I began. "He came from the shtetl of Knyszyn midway between Bialystok and Grodno, and he arrived in Chicago in 1903 with less than three dollars."

"1903 was a great year to get out," the Rabbi interjected with a smile. "Congratulations. There was a huge pogrom there the next year. If he had waited any longer he might not have made it out alive."

"That's right," I agreed. "When he got to Chicago, he changed his name to Samuel Friedman and married a woman named Jenny Pinckovitch whose sisters married into the Patinkin family. The actor, Mandy, is my second cousin, I think."

"Yes, I have met Mandy," the Rabbi said.

"So Kasiel, or Sam, whatever you want to call him, fathered six kids and died immediately afterwards. My father and his siblings were raised here in Chicago in an Orthodox orphanage called the Marks Nathan Home. My dad never forgave his mother for putting him in the Home, and to get back at her, at least in part, he subsequently married a Catholic who gave birth to me. My parents left me alone throughout my lifetime to figure out who I was, Jewish or Catholic, and where I belonged. The figuring out continues until this day."

Here I stopped to catch my breath.

Rabbi Goldberg heard me out with that warm steady smile of his as if he considered such stories routinely and many others far more complicated. He could handle this. Obviously, much to my relief, I had found the correct Rabbi. I thought, *this could be my guy.*

All of a sudden, I found myself fighting off tears.

"So that's it, Rabbi." I said. "Can you find room for me in this enormous Temple of yours?"

Rabbi Goldberg explained to me the difference between matrilineal, patrilineal, and equilineal descent, and that Liberal Judaism recognizes equilineal descent, namely, that individuals born of a Jewish father and non-Jewish mother should be treated exactly the same as individuals born to a Jewish mother and non-Jewish father. There is no certificate, no conversion process required in cases like this, like mine. "Thirty or forty years ago this would not be possible," he said, "but it is now."

The guys on the golf course were right about me all along. I was a Jew—I am a Jew—and I should have an opinion about Netanyahu and the Knesset. I didn't need shots or papers. The Rabbi didn't have to wave a wand over my head. I could show up at Temple and start being Jewish. Come as you are. I was welcome.

"You are what you do," Rabbi Goldberg said. "If you come and practice Judaism, well, then you are a Jew."

"Being here," I told him, "makes me feel connected to my father and grandfather."

"All the more reason to come," he said with a warm smile and a nod, sealing the deal.

It turns out I am already a Jew, I have always been a Jew, even though I thought I had lost my Jewishness along the way, or tried to lose it. I am one of the great Jews of all time. It's about time to embrace it. I may be a lapsed, watered-down Jew, but I am a Jew nonetheless, a Jew to my core.

When I look north along the vast expanse of Lake Michigan from the windows in my minimalist Miesian apartment at any time of day or night, I see the unrelenting flow of traffic in both directions on Lake Shore Drive, the jetties and apartment blocks at North Avenue, Fullerton, and Belmont Harbor, the air traffic stacked up flying westward into O'Hare, and I always think first of my father, Dan, in his customary pose, behind the wheel of his car going somewhere in a hurry, fat tires thumping at highway speed against the pavement. He's out there, dressed warmly, wearing the brown flat cap he favored as he got older, and his lined corduroy winter jacket and black leather gloves, smiling, driving into the glare of the winter sun.

Here in Chicago, my father is always with me.

Epilogue

Yad Vashem

On August 2, 2016, in Jerusalem, the day after my sixty-fifth birthday, I went to Yad Vashem, Israel's great monument to the Holocaust, which they call in Hebrew the Shoah, or the "destruction." It is a terribly powerful place. I wept from one end of it to the other before I couldn't take it anymore.

In the Hall of Names, I sat behind a computer monitor and accessed its vast online archive of people killed by the Nazis and their collaborators. I typed into the database the name Skolnick and the place Knyszyn, and several entries immediately appeared on the screen, shocking me. Someone had submitted Pages of Testimony about my family to Yad Vashem.

Kasiel Skolnick, my grandfather, fled luckless Knyszyn in 1903, but his younger brother Kalman Skolnick, a grain merchant, had stayed. Kalman's wife, Khaia, and their three daughters, Ida, Ester, and Khana, were listed in the archive as "murdered."

Under each name was the same notation: "Prior to World War II she lived in Knyszyn, Poland. During the war she was in Knyszyn, Poland. She was murdered in the Shoah."

I sat in the Hall of Names with my wife and I wept. Through my tears, the elderly clerk next to us at the reference desk looked like my grandmother Jenny, Kasiel's wife, my father's mother. I looked over at her and said: "they were all murdered." She did not respond so I stared at her and repeated: "they were all murdered." I did not know what I was asking for, or expected, but I wanted to share with her this news. This time she shrugged at me, but not without compassion. I can't imagine what she must see in the Hall of Names. Many must come in every day, take a seat behind a terminal, type in a family and place name, and receive the truth.

One brother decided to leave, one brother decided to stay. We were that close to not making it. Tiny, unknown, impoverished, trailblazing Kasiel Skolnick, our Grandpa Sam, finally acknowledged under a new headstone in Waldheim Cemetery, thank God for your daring, vigilance, and impeccable timing. Without you, we would not have had the chance to live.

Acknowledgments

Glenn Lee Friedman, son of my uncle Si, documented our family history on his personal website long before the rest of us were even vaguely interested in the subject. Glenn died in 2010. His son, Dan, the father of five and a computer engineer, restored for us his father's vanished computer files, bringing all of his stories and photos of the Friedman orphans back to life.

On his own, Greg Friedman found the blank slab at Waldheim Cemetery that covered his grandfather's grave. Greg took up a symbolic collection among his cousins and had the grave re-marked with a proper headstone with our grandfather's chosen American name, "Samuel Friedman." Greg told me he was motivated to do so by the birth of his first grandchild.

Carola Murray-Seegert is a skilled genealogist living in Germany and a Friedman by marriage. Carola found the manifest of the SS *Breslau* and the name of a certain passenger of great interest to us, a twenty-two-year-old Hebrew tailor named Kasiel Skolnick.

Barbara Chandler, Senior Development Associate at Jewish Child & Family Services in Chicago, showed me every document in the agency's possession pertaining to the Marks Nathan Home, including the *Oral History Project* compiled by Aaron Gruenberg. Kathy Bloch, a librarian at the Spertus Institute for Jewish Learning and Leadership in Chicago, located and made photocopies for me of documents I had never seen, and did not know existed, including my father's birth certificate, and his original application, age five, for admittance to the Marks Nathan Home. Marsha Raynes, Manager of Project Esther: the Chicago Jewish Adoption Network, a program of Jewish Child & Family Services in Skokie, spent time helping me interpret the documents and fully understand them. I am grateful to Barbara, Kathy, and Marsha for their expertise, kindness, and support.

I owe thanks to Susan Baron, who invited me to her home and shared with me many stories of her father's childhood in the Marks Nathan Home. Susan inherited all of her father's charm and optimism, and four three-ring binders of Home memorabilia, the only remains from all those years on South Albany Avenue.

At Skyhorse Publishing I thank Mark Gompertz, Joe Craig, and Olga Greco.

My wife, Margaret Scott Dallas Friedman, gave me the courage and love I needed to see this important story through to the end. She believed in me—and it—every step of the way. For that I am most grateful.

Select Bibliography

Nelson Algren: *Chicago: City on the Make* (University of Chicago Press, 1951).
Martin Amis: *Experience* (Random House, 2000).
Saul Bellow: *The Adventures of Augie March* (Weidenfeld & Nicholson, 1954).
Saul Bellow: *Ravelstein* (Penguin, 2000).
Ian Buruma: *Their Promised Land: My Grandparents in Love and War* (Penguin, 2016).
Roald Dahl: *Danny the Champion of the World* (Puffin Books, 1975).
Junot Diaz: *This Is How You Lose Her* (Riverhead Books, 2012).
Edmund de Waal: *The Hare with Amber Eyes* (Farrar, Straus & Giroux, 2010).
Thomas Dyja: *The Third Coast* (Penguin, 2013).
Erik Larson: *The Devil in the White City* (Random House, 2003).
Marceline Loridan-Ivens: *But You Did Not Come Back* (Atlantic Monthly Press, 2016).

Irène Némirovsky: *Suite Française* (Random House, 2006).
Irène Némirovsky: *The Fires of Autumn* (Random House, 2015).
Philip Roth: *Patrimony* (Random House, 1991).
Geoffrey Wolff: *The Duke of Deception: Memoirs of My Father* (Random House, 1979).

Made in the USA
Columbia, SC
09 March 2023